ADELE BYRNE

ACT

BREAKING FREE FROM ANXIETY, PHOBIAS, AND WORRY:
THE ULTIMATE GUIDE TO ACCEPTANCE AND COMMITMENT
THERAPY FOR OVERCOMING FEAR AND EMBRACING LIFE

TABLE OF CONTENTS

INTRODUCTION

D id you know that anxiety disorders affect over 284 million people worldwide? This staggering number highlights the urgent need for effective strategies to conquer fear and embrace a life of fulfillment.

Suffering is a universal experience that extends beyond physical or psychological pain. It encompasses difficult self-assessments, uncomfortable feelings, and painful memories. While the instinctive response is to avoid suffering, a good life encompasses more than just minimizing it. This is where Acceptance and Commitment Therapy (ACT) comes in. ACT not only focuses on understanding human suffering but also recognizes its significance in realizing a fulfilling life. As a form of Cognitive Behavioral Therapy (CBT), ACT addresses essential questions such as one's purpose in life. Before we explore ACT further, let's gain a deeper understanding of human suffering.

Pets, such as cats or dogs, find it easier to attain happiness as long as their basic needs for food, water, shelter, warmth, and play are met. However, humans, even with the abundance of modern conveniences like technology and supermarkets, can still experience misery. Stories of wealthy individuals struggling with emotional distress or resorting to harmful habits highlight the natural presence of suffering in our lives.

Human suffering encompasses both psychological and physiological aspects. Physical pain involves the transmission of signals to the brain, alerting us to a problem in our body. The psychological aspect revolves around the meaning we assign to that pain, influenced by our beliefs and triggering emotional responses. Emotional and mental reactions to pain contribute to human suffering. Chronic pain involves both biological and psychological components that work together, acting as a radar to monitor our psychological well-being.

While we cannot eliminate pain, we can choose our response to suffering, just as we can choose how to respond to anger. Pain serves as a function that notifies us of imbalances in our physical, mental, and spiritual dimensions. Any disruption in one dimension can affect others, necessitating the restoration of balance. Human suffering is both a cause and effect of distressing emotions such as helplessness, loneliness, depression, and anxiety. Negative thinking exacerbates the perception of situations and can become self-defeating and self-fulfilling.

For those experiencing chronic pain, there is a direct link between pain levels and negative thinking, leading to a dangerous cycle. Pain triggers negative thoughts and self-doubt, which generate emotions aligned with human suffering. This experience increases stress and muscle tension, intensifying the pain signals. This negative progression perpetuates a vicious cycle, leaving individuals increasingly imbalanced.

To break free from this cycle, it is essential to develop awareness and learn to respond differently to pain. The recovery process involves modifying the negative progression, starting with cognitive and emotional balance through mindfulness and acceptance strategies. By restoring balance, individuals can counteract the negative dynamics and detach from their pain. This leads to decreased negative emotions, reduced muscle tension, and diminished stress.

Although the process is challenging, it is entirely possible with effort and commitment. By adjusting our thoughts and reshaping our emotional responses, including our ability to tolerate suffering, we can effectively address and alleviate human suffering.

Imagine a young professional yearning to navigate social anxiety and thrive in their career. Picture a mother burdened by constant worry, longing to savor the precious moments with her children. Envision a student struggling with paralyzing phobias, dreaming of a life filled with boundless opportunities. This book is for those seeking liberation from the grip of fear, individuals who yearn to embrace life's joys with open arms.

Before you continue reading this book, it's important to assess if it aligns with your needs and aspirations. This handbook is not for those seeking quick fixes or easy solutions without a willingness to invest time and effort. It is not intended for individuals resistant to change or personal growth, who prefer to remain stagnant in their current state. If you are not open to exploring your emotions, confronting fears, and engaging in introspection, this resource may not be the right fit for you. Additionally, it goes beyond addressing specific phobias or anxieties and requires a broader interest in personal development. This book expects active participation, self-reflection, and a readiness to challenge beliefs. Take a moment to reflect on your readiness to embark on a transformative journey of self-discovery and growth.

For those who doubt the power of words to catalyze change, let this book be your testament. Within these pages, you will find the tools, insights, and inspiration needed to transcend your fears and step boldly into a life of authenticity and fulfillment. Open your heart and mind, and embrace the possibility that awaits you.

In a sea of self-help books, this resource stands out as a beacon of hope, offering more than mere words on a page. As you journey through its pages, you'll find a tapestry woven with evidence-based techniques that dig deep into the very core of our human experience. It courageously explores the profound emotional, psychological, and spiritual dimensions of our struggles, inviting you to confront your fears head-on. Prepare to be enthralled, pushed beyond your comfort zone, and ultimately liberated from the grips of anxiety, phobias, and worry.

Continue reading, embark on this journey, and unlock the secrets that will transform your relationship with fear. With each chapter, you'll gain invaluable knowledge, practical techniques, and a renewed sense of hope. Embrace the adventure that lies ahead and seize the opportunity to live a life unbounded by anxiety. Your transformation begins now.

CHAPTER 1: EXPLORING THE FOUNDATIONS OF ACCEPTANCE AND COMMITMENT THERAPY

Acceptance and Commitment Therapy (ACT) is an innovative therapeutic approach that integrates mindfulness practice and cognitive behavioral psychotherapy, offering individuals a powerful framework for personal growth and transformation. What sets ACT apart from traditional cognitive behavioral therapy is its distinctive emphasis on changing the relationship with thoughts, rather than trying to directly modify the thoughts themselves.

In ACT, the aim is to cultivate psychological flexibility, which involves developing an open and accepting attitude towards one's thoughts, emotions, and sensations. Mindfulness serves as a foundational element of ACT, enabling individuals to observe their internal experiences with curiosity and non-judgment. Through mindfulness, individuals gain a deeper awareness of their thoughts and emotions, allowing them to disengage from unhelpful patterns and create space for more adaptive responses.

Another key component of ACT is the diffusion of challenging thoughts. Rather than attempting to eliminate or control unwanted thoughts, ACT teaches individuals techniques to distance themselves from the content of their thoughts. By recognizing thoughts as mental events rather than absolute truths, individuals can reduce the impact and influence of negative thinking patterns.

Additionally, ACT emphasizes the acceptance of unpleasant emotions, recognizing that discomfort and distress are natural parts of the human experience. Instead of avoiding or suppressing these emotions, ACT encourages individuals to embrace them fully and make room for them in their lives. This acceptance enables individuals to shift their focus towards actions that align with their deeply-held values and create a sense of meaning and purpose.

Through committed action and a shift in perspective, ACT empowers individuals to break free from the constraints of their thoughts and emotions, enabling them to live more fully in the present moment. By aligning their actions with their values, individuals can create a life that is rich in purpose and fulfillment. ACT provides practical tools and techniques to support individuals in their journey towards a more authentic and meaningful existence, helping them develop resilience, enhance relationships, and cultivate psychological well-being.

Acceptance and Commitment Therapy encompasses three fundamental mindfulness skills that are categorized as follows:

Acceptance: This essential skill in ACT enables individuals to create a spacious and non-judgmental mindset towards their sensations, urges, and painful feelings. By embracing acceptance, individuals can allow these experiences to naturally arise and pass without attempting to control or suppress them. This acceptance-based approach fosters psychological flexibility and empowers individuals to engage with life more fully.

Defusion: The defusion skill in ACT empowers individuals to detach themselves from unhelpful thoughts, memories, and beliefs. It involves recognizing that thoughts are not necessarily accurate reflections of reality but rather mental events that can be observed and let go of. By developing a sense of distance from their thoughts, individuals can reduce their influence over their actions and emotions, freeing themselves to align their behavior with their values.

Contact with the present moment: This skill encourages individuals to engage fully with their present experience, cultivating a sense of curiosity and openness. By immersing themselves in the here and now, individuals can deepen their connection to their surroundings, their inner selves, and the richness of each moment. This heightened awareness of the present moment enhances clarity, self-understanding, and the ability to make conscious choices aligned with personal values.

ACT can be implemented in various formats to accommodate different needs and treatment contexts:

Ultra-brief ACT: Even in as little as one or two twenty to thirty-minute sessions, ACT can have a profound impact. This approach has been successfully utilized by Kirk Strosahl, co-founder of ACT, in primary care medical settings, demonstrating the effectiveness of ACT in brief encounters.

Brief ACT: With just four one-hour sessions, ACT has shown effectiveness in treating individuals with conditions such as schizophrenia. Patty Bach, assistant professor of psychology at the Illinois Institute of Technology, has employed this time-limited approach with positive outcomes, emphasizing the potential for meaningful change within a short timeframe.

Medium-term ACT: An eight-hour protocol, developed by JoAnne Dahl, professor of psychology at Uppsala University in Sweden, has demonstrated promise in managing chronic pain. This medium-term approach provides more extensive exploration and practice of ACT techniques, offering individuals a deeper understanding of their experiences and enhanced coping skills.

Long-term ACT: Specifically designed for individuals with Borderline Personality Disorder (BPD), long-term ACT involves forty two-hour sessions. Spectrum, the Personality Disorder Service in Victoria, Australia, is among the few known providers of this comprehensive treatment option. This extended treatment duration allows for a thorough exploration of the complexities associated with BPD and provides ample time for significant personal growth and transformation.

These diverse delivery methods highlight the adaptability and effectiveness of ACT across a range of therapeutic contexts and patient populations. By tailoring the duration and intensity of ACT to meet individual needs, practitioners can maximize its potential for positive change and empower individuals to live more meaningful and fulfilling lives.

The Impact of Therapy on the Brain

Decades of research, as highlighted in a 1998 study published in the American Journal of Psychology, have established that all mental processes originate from brain mechanisms. This means that any changes in our psychological functioning are mirrored by corresponding alterations in brain function or structure. Consequently, it is no surprise that the outcomes and effects of therapeutic interventions, which facilitate change within individuals, have been extensively examined at both social and psychological levels. These changes, encompassing improvements in social functioning, personality, psychological abilities, and symptom reduction, are essentially manifestations of underlying brain mechanisms.

Acceptance and Commitment Therapy a distinctive branch of Cognitive Behavioral Therapy (CBT), offers a unique approach to addressing a wide range of symptoms. Unlike conventional therapies, ACT seeks to identify the non-physical causes of mental disorders, recognizing that experiences such as depression, addictions, obsessive-compulsive disorder, and schizophrenia emerge from multifaceted factors. It takes into account genetic, epigenetic (not inherited through DNA), psychological, and cultural conditions. Employing a syndrome-based strategy, ACT identifies clusters of symptoms as syndromes linked to specific sets of conditions (Hayes and Lillis, 2012, 5).

Initially conceptualized by Steven Hayes in 1980, ACT was subsequently developed into a comprehensive therapeutic model by his students and colleagues, notably Kirk Strosahl and Kelly Wilson, in 1999 (ibid, xv). These researchers were driven by the desire to find more effective ways of alleviating human suffering and assisting individuals in navigating relational and daily life challenges. They were perplexed by the prevalence of human suffering, even in circumstances of material wealth and success. Recognizing the importance of delving into root causes rather than merely addressing symptoms, Hayes and his team adopted an inductive and process-oriented approach to understanding human distress and failure, taking into consideration the unique context of each case (ibid, 6).

Despite its potential, Acceptance and Commitment Therapy initially encountered limited adoption among therapists until the turn of the millennium (ibid, 15). This can be attributed to the widespread popularity and dominance of Cognitive Behavioral Therapy (CBT) throughout the 20th century. CBT, with its focus on restructuring maladaptive thoughts and behaviors, enjoyed significant recognition and support within the mental health field.

However, as the years progressed, a growing recognition of the limitations of CBT began to emerge. While CBT demonstrated effectiveness in certain cases, it often fell short when it came to addressing the complexities of human experience and the range of mental health challenges individuals face. The emphasis on modifying thoughts and behaviors sometimes overlooked the deeper emotional and existential aspects of psychological well-being.

During this time, Acceptance and Commitment Therapy quietly continued to evolve and refine its approach. ACT presented a fresh perspective, moving beyond the narrow focus on symptom reduction and instead embracing a broader understanding of human suffering. It acknowledged that mental health challenges stem from a complex interplay of genetic, environmental, and psychological factors, and sought to address the root causes rather than merely alleviating symptoms.

As therapists and researchers delved deeper into the principles and techniques of ACT, they began to witness its transformative impact firsthand. ACT demonstrated efficacy in addressing a wide range of mental health issues, including anxiety, depression, substance abuse, eating disorders, and chronic pain. Its emphasis on psychological flexibility, mindfulness, and values-driven action resonated with both therapists and individuals seeking more comprehensive and meaningful approaches to mental well-being.

As a result, ACT gained momentum and recognition within the mental health community. Therapists and researchers started incorporating ACT into their practice, and its evidence-based effectiveness continued to grow. The increasing body of research supporting ACT's efficacy further fueled its rise to prominence, establishing it as a viable and valuable therapeutic approach for addressing the diverse and nuanced challenges of mental health in the modern era.

Evolution of Therapeutic Perspectives: From Behaviorism to Acceptance and Commitment Therapy

During the 1960s, behavioral therapy gained popularity as it placed a strong emphasis on empiricism and the need for measurable outcomes in psychological interventions. This approach focused on external stimuli and observable behaviors, with limited attention given to the intricate complexities of human experience. The theoretical foundations of this early behavioral therapy were mainly derived from humanism and psychoanalysis, which resulted in misdiagnoses and oversimplification of psychological issues (Hayes and Lillis, 2012, 16).

As a reaction to the shortcomings of purely behavioral approaches and a desire to move away from the excessive reliance on analytical symbolism, Acceptance and Commitment Therapy emerged as a more integrative and unconventional therapeutic approach. While still rooted in behavioral therapy, ACT integrated elements from psychoanalytical and humanistic perspectives. It recognized the significance of exploring the underlying human issues that contribute to problematic behavior (ibid, 18).

The limitations of behaviorism became evident as it failed to consider higher-level cognitive processes such as language, meaning, conceptualization, and symbolism. The exclusive focus on externally observable factors in controlled laboratory conditions ignored the intricate internal workings of the mind (ibid). On the other hand, cognitive psychology emerged to address cognitive processes but faced challenges in translating its theories into practical results and lacked substantial evidence for its models. However, cognitive therapy began to develop as therapists engaged in meaningful conversations with patients, helping them recognize and self-direct their behavioral errors (ibid, 20). As a result, alternative approaches started to gain attention.

Acceptance and commitment therapists recognized the need for a more comprehensive understanding of human behavior and aimed to bridge the gap between behavioral and cognitive approaches. They acknowledged the limitations of strict behavior modification and emphasized the importance of addressing cognitive processes and underlying human issues. By integrating acceptance, mindfulness, and values-driven action, ACT emerged as a holistic therapeutic approach. It not only sought behavioral change but also delved into the intricate social conditions that contribute to human suffering (ibid).

As the field of psychotherapy evolved, the development of ACT represented a significant shift in therapeutic perspectives, embracing a more comprehensive and nuanced understanding of human psychology. This integrative approach laid the foundation for ACT to become a recognized and effective therapeutic model for a wide range of mental health challenges. Its emphasis on acceptance, mindfulness, and values-driven action has allowed ACT to address the underlying complexities of human experience and promote lasting change and well-being.

ACT: Embracing Experiential Psychotherapy

ACT, a contemporary form of Cognitive Behavioral Therapy, has garnered significant attention in recent years. It diverges from traditional approaches by placing emphasis on values, acceptance, mindfulness, and processes that empower individuals to overcome life's obstacles.

Central to ACT is the understanding that human suffering is an inherent part of the human experience. It recognizes that people often engage in futile attempts to control or avoid their own experiences, which can ultimately lead to further distress and dissatisfaction. ACT offers effective strategies for managing pain, cultivating mindfulness, gaining clarity on personal values, and pursuing a life of deeper meaning. Rather than seeking to eliminate pain altogether, the goal of ACT is to teach individuals how to navigate life's challenges with greater ease and resilience.

ACT, renowned for its evidence-based approach, stands as a cornerstone of empirical psychotherapy, driven by a steadfast dedication to scientific advancement and the meticulous assessment of its origins and effects. Since 2014, ACT has undergone extensive scrutiny through over 80 rigorous randomized clinical trials, encompassing a diverse cohort of more than 5,000 participants. These studies have delved into the efficacy of ACT across a wide spectrum of concerns, illuminating its potential to address various psychological challenges.

The robust empirical foundation of ACT has not only solidified its status as a therapeutic model but has also catalyzed its expansion into other domains. Beyond the realms of traditional therapy, ACT has engendered the development of Acceptance and Commitment Training (ACTr), a non-therapeutic application that focuses on honing essential skills related to values, acceptance, and mindfulness. ACTr serves as a valuable resource for individuals seeking personal growth, enhancing their capacity to navigate life's complexities, and fostering a sense of well-being and fulfillment.

The growth and diversification of ACT, evident in its extensive research and the emergence of ACTr, exemplify the far-reaching impact of this profound therapeutic approach. By prioritizing scientific rigor and continuously expanding its application, ACT continues to unlock new possibilities for promoting psychological well-being and facilitating personal transformation.

Relational Frame Theory: Understanding the Link Between Language and Behavior

Relational Frame Theory (RFT) forms the conceptual underpinning of ACT, providing a comprehensive framework to understand the intricate relationship between human behavior and language. RFT delves into the exploration of how language influences our thoughts, emotions, and actions.

Language holds a pivotal role in psychotherapy as it serves as the medium through which we engage in private thoughts and public interactions. It allows us to think, speak, evaluate, categorize, describe, and relate to the world around us. Language has been instrumental in the development of human civilization, enabling the establishment of laws and societal rules that regulate our behavior.

While language offers immense benefits, it also has its darker side. Like the yin and yang, it possesses both powerful positive and negative aspects. According to RFT, language plays a critical role in human suffering. It can be used to form prejudiced assumptions, harbor negative thoughts, obsess over events, and revisit past traumas. Excessive use of language and incessant thinking can hinder our ability to stay present, as we become consumed by thoughts of the past or worries about the future, thereby impairing our capacity to fully enjoy the present moment.

By delving deeper into the mechanisms of human language, RFT aims to harness its positive aspects while mitigating the impact of its negative aspects. This understanding forms the foundation of RFT within the context of ACT, providing valuable insights for psychotherapists seeking to address psychological issues.

When studying how human language influences behavior, researchers often focus on two key aspects: generativity and symbolism. Symbolism refers to the use of language to represent objects or ideas, where specific words carry meaning. For example, the word "tree" symbolizes a type of plant with a trunk, branches, and leaves. Understanding the meaning behind words allows for effective communication.

Generativity, on the other hand, pertains to our ability to create and understand an infinite number of meaningful sentences. It reflects the productivity of language. While languages have a finite set of letters, sounds, and words, each individual can generate countless unique sentences using these linguistic elements.

Different theories have been developed to explore these linguistic features, often highlighting specific properties or focusing on particular concerns. Linguists attribute the novelty and complexity of language to genetic factors, whereas cognitive psychologists emphasize the role of the brain in processing and storing information, including symbols. Despite these variations, most language studies share the common understanding that language serves as a system of symbols that allows us to express our ideas and be understood by others.

In contrast to traditional approaches, RFT takes a distinct methodological stance in understanding language and cognition. Instead of viewing language as a means of communication between individuals, RFT focuses on how humans acquire language through interactions with people and their environment. This perspective provides a practical and useful analysis of language and cognition, moving beyond mere description.

ACT, as the applied technology of RFT, aims to assist individuals in utilizing language as a tool to address specific psychological issues. It employs the psychological flexibility model, which forms a unique aspect of ACT, to promote adaptive responses to challenging thoughts and emotions. By embracing a comprehensive understanding of language and cognition, ACT empowers individuals to enhance their psychological flexibility and navigate the complexities of their inner experiences.

The Psychological Flexibility Model: Cultivating Resilience, Authenticity, and Values-Based Living

At the heart of Acceptance and Commitment Therapy lies the profound goal of enhancing psychological flexibility—a vital skill that empowers individuals to navigate life's challenges with resilience and authenticity. Psychological flexibility encompasses our capacity to remain present, fully aware, and adaptable in any given situation, all while aligning our behaviors with our deeply held values. It requires us to hold our thoughts and emotions lightly, recognizing their impermanence, and making choices guided by our long-term values rather than being swayed by fleeting impulses or momentary feelings.

In the fast-paced and demanding world we live in, it is easy to get caught up in the rollercoaster of emotions and the incessant chatter of our minds. However, ACT encourages us to step back, observe our thoughts and emotions without judgment, and avoid being controlled by them. By creating distance from our internal experiences, we gain a clearer perspective and can make conscious choices that align with our core values and aspirations. This shift allows us to identify the emerging patterns of action that lead to growth and fulfillment, helping us discover authentic meaning in our lives and experience the richness that life has to offer.

To measure psychological flexibility, the widely used Acceptance and Action Questionnaire provides valuable insights for psychotherapists and ACT specialists. This comprehensive questionnaire helps predict various psychological concerns, including depression, poor work performance, substance abuse, anxiety sensitivity, long-term disability, higher anxiety levels, general pathology, alexithymia (difficulty in identifying and expressing emotions), and excessive worry. By understanding an individual's level of psychological flexibility, practitioners can tailor ACT interventions to address specific needs and promote well-being effectively.

The Psychological Flexibility Model encompasses six core processes that serve as the building blocks of psychological flexibility. These processes—Acceptance, Cognitive Defusion, Being Present, Self-as-Context, Values, and Committed Action—empower individuals to develop essential psychological skills. It is important to note that these processes are not intended as quick-fix techniques to resolve psychological issues but rather as positive skills that foster psychological flexibility and facilitate values-based living. In the forthcoming chapter, we will explore each of these processes in depth, highlighting their significance in cultivating resilience, authenticity, and a life guided by one's deepest values.

Navigating the ACT Journey: Overcoming Challenges and Embracing Growth

Embarking on the journey of life, much like engaging in Acceptance and Commitment Therapy, involves a dynamic and ever-changing process filled with a multitude of experiences. Along this path, it is crucial to be aware of the common challenges and pitfalls that individuals may encounter while living an ACT-inspired life. Understanding and addressing these challenges will empower you to stay motivated, resilient, and open to the growth that awaits you.

Embracing Patience: Trusting the Process

Impatience can often surface when we yearn for instant outcomes, mirroring the impatience of a preschooler learning to tie their shoes. In the realm of Acceptance and Commitment Therapy, it is natural to feel frustrated at times, questioning why the desired results are not achieved quickly. However, it is essential to recognize that ACT is not a quick-fix solution; it is an ongoing odyssey, akin to the journey of learning to tie your shoes. Just as mastering the art of shoe-tying requires time, practice, and patience, so does the cultivation of a values-driven life. By embracing patience and understanding that genuine change takes time, you lay the foundation for long-term growth and a profound transformation of your life.

Mindful Progress: Avoiding the Need for Speed

Commencing your odyssey towards creating a high-quality life is undeniably exhilarating. However, it is vital to strike a delicate balance and avoid setting unrealistic, short-term goals. The key lies in immersing yourself in the learning process, dedicating ample time to comprehend the core concepts of ACT, and actively engaging with the exercises provided. By allowing yourself the necessary time to absorb this wisdom, you equip yourself with the knowledge and skills required to take more effective and sustainable action as your journey unfolds. Rushing forward without a solid foundation can lead to stumbling and setbacks, much like a child hastily tying shoelaces only to trip and fall when the laces come undone. Remember, true progress is not measured by speed alone but by the depth and authenticity of your growth.

Conquering Hesitation: Striking a Balance

Finding the delicate balance in goal-setting is crucial during your ACT journey. While it is important to challenge yourself and aspire to meaningful achievements, it is equally vital to avoid setting goals that are grandiose and overwhelming for your current stage. Fear of failure or unfavorable outcomes may give rise to hesitation, prompting us to retreat into the safety of our comfort zones. However, reflecting on the analogy of learning to tie your shoes as a child can provide valuable insight. Imagine if you had indefinitely postponed the task, fearing the unknown. Progress would have remained elusive. To overcome the pitfall of hesitation, it is essential to set goals that stretch your capabilities while still being within reach. Each goal should be approached with a clear understanding of how its achievement will propel you forward on your journey, igniting a chain reaction of growth and self-discovery.

By recognizing and addressing the pitfalls of impatience, excessive speed, and hesitation, you empower yourself to navigate the ACT journey with resilience and purpose. Embrace patience as a guiding companion, maintaining a mindful pace that allows for deep understanding and integration of the principles of ACT. Set goals that strike the delicate balance between challenge and achievability, ensuring continuous progress and meaningful transformation. Remember, every step forward, no matter how small, brings you closer to a life of authenticity, fulfillment, and alignment with your core values. Embrace the transformative power of ACT, trust in the process, and embark on this extraordinary journey of self-discovery and growth.

CHAPTER 2: THE CORE PROCESSES OF ACCEPTANCE AND COMMITMENT THERAPY

I n ACT, the focus revolves around the six core processes that center on psychological flexibility. These processes, which work in harmony rather than as isolated techniques for psychotherapy, are crucial for framing our thoughts in an expansive way. Let's explore each of these processes with empathy and understanding.

Acceptance

Acceptance is a distinctive approach that counters experiential avoidance, encouraging individuals to consciously and actively embrace their personal history without attempting to alter its form or frequency. This process acknowledges the importance of safeguarding one's psychological well-being, even if it means refraining from altering certain aspects of one's experiences.

For instance, individuals grappling with anxiety are encouraged to acknowledge anxiety as a natural human emotion. Similarly, those dealing with chronic pain are guided towards specific treatments to help them cope effectively. It is important to note that this process is not an endpoint in itself but rather a means to foster value-based actions.

At first, individuals suffering from anxiety may find it perplexing when ACT specialists suggest accepting something that has been causing them distress. It may seem counterintuitive, prompting questions such as, "Why should we accept anxiety? Doesn't that mean we have to live with this harmful emotion?"

However, this is the essence of ACT. The process entails acceptance, followed by the readiness to move forward. While it may sound contradictory, letting go of something after acceptance is possible. Language serves as a representation, and there are instances when it signifies more than the literal meaning. Acceptance, in its most literal sense, refers to receiving something.

Traditional mental health practitioners often advocated for acceptance as a way to learn how to coexist with an issue like anxiety. However, this perspective could prove detrimental, potentially causing internal conflicts, confusion, and exacerbating anxiety symptoms. From an ACT standpoint, acceptance and letting go involve transforming something into an object that supports a more meaningful life. This shift in thinking not only empowers individuals but also weakens the grip of anxiety. Similar to anger, anxiety derives its strength from our responses to it. In the context of ACT, acceptance entails suspending judgment and cultivating heightened self-awareness, as if observing ourselves from an external perspective.

Letting go of anxiety can occur naturally when we refrain from judgment and fear. If we remain unaware of negative thoughts, we inadvertently reinforce our attachment to things that could harm us. While it may seem like self-protection to avoid negative emotions, the earnest effort to eliminate something can paradoxically intensify our attachment to it.

Practice Mindfulness

You don't have to possess the deep wisdom of a monk or be a master of meditation to embrace the practice of mindfulness and experience its profound effects. It's a practice accessible to everyone, including you, my friend. Let's explore the simple yet profound joy of being fully present and cultivate a deeper sense of awareness together.

Start by savoring the exquisite pleasure of a mindful breakfast. Set aside distractions and immerse yourself in the experience. Feel the warmth of each sip of coffee as it envelops your senses, relish the bittersweet taste that dances on your tongue, and inhale the delightful aroma that fills the air. Engage all your senses, allowing the present moment to unfold its wonders. Try to incorporate this mindful approach into your daily routine, beginning with a simple activity that you regularly engage in.

Now, let's gently guide our attention back to the simplicity of life whenever our minds wander. When you catch your thoughts drifting, be kind to yourself and gently regain focus. Choose something ordinary and monotonous in your surroundings—a piece of paper, a cup of coffee, or even the touch of your own hand. Focus your attention on these simple objects, free from triggering emotions. Let them serve as gentle reminders to bring your awareness back to the present moment. Each time you find yourself daydreaming, repeat this practice until you naturally transition back to the task at hand.

Remember the wondrous sense of wonder we experienced as children when time seemed to pass slowly? As we embarked on new adventures, we fully immersed ourselves in the present moment, eagerly embracing every new experience. Let's recapture that spirit by incorporating novelty into our daily lives. Engage in new activities, big or small, and observe how our attention is captivated. Embrace the learning process that comes with new endeavors, allowing ourselves to be fully present as we navigate uncharted territory.

In our fast-paced world, it's all too easy to get caught up in the habit of always looking forward, anticipating future outcomes and trying to stay one step ahead. However, by constantly allowing our minds to wander, we miss out on the precious moments that make life truly meaningful. While planning is essential, dwelling on countless hypothetical scenarios that may never come to pass can hinder our ability to fully experience the beauty of the present.

Let us gently release the need for constant prediction and instead cultivate a deep appreciation for the here and now. Embrace the richness of each moment, for it is in these fleeting instances that life truly unfolds. By nurturing mindfulness, we can navigate the delicate balance of being prepared while wholeheartedly embracing the wonders of the present. Let's embark on this journey together, cherishing the precious moments and discovering the profound beauty that lies in the art of being fully present.

Cognitive Defusion

In the journey of ACT, we are encouraged to practice cognitive defusion, which involves detaching ourselves from harmful thinking patterns. It's important to recognize that we all have a tendency to become overly attached to our thoughts, often magnifying their impact on us. However, we can learn to accept the truth that thoughts are simply thoughts. This understanding doesn't undermine the emotional weight they can carry or their role in enhancing our awareness. It's about acknowledging that thoughts only hold as much power as we allow them to have. They are like passing words and images in our mind, and it is up to us to assign meaning to them.

We don't always have to react immediately to our thoughts, especially when they are strong or distressing. When intrusive thoughts arise or persist, it's beneficial to apply acceptance and mindfulness principles before taking any actions based on them. Cognitive defusion invites us to observe our thoughts rather than becoming entangled in them, to look at our thoughts rather than through them, and to let thoughts come and go without clinging onto them.

Through the practice of cognitive defusion, we can recognize that thoughts are merely mental constructs generated by our emotions. By observing their essence, we can respond to our thoughts in a way that aligns with what actually works for us. This is where mindfulness plays a significant role. It helps us become aware when we are excessively attached to our thoughts, allowing us to free ourselves from their influence on our behavior.

Cognitive defusion is particularly useful when we want to challenge thoughts that hinder us from living a values-based life. It enables us to assess our response to thoughts and empowers us to make conscious choices that support our well-being and growth.

One of the most empowering aspects of cognitive defusion is its ability to help us assess our responses to these hindering thoughts. It encourages us to step back and observe our thoughts from a place of curiosity and non-judgment. Instead of automatically accepting them as absolute truths or allowing them to dictate our actions, we can take a moment to pause, reflect, and consciously choose our next steps.

This process of assessment and conscious choice is transformative. It allows us to recognize the thoughts that no longer serve us and make intentional decisions that support our well-being and personal growth. By disentangling ourselves from the grip of negative or limiting thoughts, we create space for more positive and empowering ones to emerge.

It's important to note that cognitive defusion doesn't imply that all thoughts are inherently harmful. Our human capacity to think and make sense of our thoughts adds richness to our lives. However, certain thinking patterns can become detrimental when they generate significant tension or stress. By cultivating awareness of our thoughts and developing a healthy distance from them, we can diminish their perceived strength and regain control over our lives.

Self as Context

Within the intricate tapestry of human language, there exist relational frames that shape our perception of self and the world around us. Concepts such as Here vs. There, Now vs. Then, and I vs. You contribute to the rich tapestry of our humanity, allowing us to transcend the physical and delve into the realm of the spiritual.

This understanding forms a fundamental pillar of both Relational Frame Theory (RFT) and Acceptance and Commitment Therapy. Over time, progressive evidence has illuminated the significance of self as context in various facets of our cognitive functioning, including the development of a sense of self, theory of mind, and empathy.

In the context of ACT, self as context plays a vital role. It empowers individuals to cultivate awareness of their own flow of experiences without becoming entangled in attachments or rigid self-identifications. Through experiential processes, the use of metaphors, and mindfulness exercises, ACT fosters the development of self as context.

At the heart of this core process lies mindfulness—the seed from which self as context blossoms. By nurturing a mindful connection with our senses, we sharpen our ability to observe ourselves and the intricacies of our human experience. Through this lens, we gain a deeper understanding of our personal growth and our place in life's journey. We become attuned to the influence of our upbringing and how it shapes our present moment, as well as the potential impact it may have on our future.

Mindfulness serves as a critical cornerstone within the framework of ACT, warranting a dedicated chapter to its exploration. It invites us to immerse ourselves in the present moment, fully embracing the richness of our sensory experiences and cultivating a compassionate awareness of our inner landscape. By embracing mindfulness, we lay the groundwork for the transformative power of self as context to unfold, enabling us to navigate life's challenges with greater clarity, acceptance, and resilience.

Remember, the journey of self as context and mindfulness is an ongoing practice, one that requires patience, dedication, and self-compassion. As you delve deeper into this process, you will uncover profound insights about yourself and your place in the world. Embrace this transformative journey, and may it empower you to cultivate a more profound connection with your inner self and navigate life's intricacies with greater wisdom and authenticity.

Values

In the realm of cognitive behavior, values are the specific qualities that inspire and motivate purposeful action. These values provide a compass for navigating life's journey and making choices aligned with what truly matters to you.

As you embark on your journey of Acceptance and Commitment Therapy (ACT), your specialist will encourage you to engage in exercises that facilitate the exploration of your values across various domains, such as career, family, and spirituality. These exercises serve as transformative tools to challenge the influence of verbal processes that may lead you astray, relying on attachments, social conformity, or avoidance to guide your decisions.

Consider, for instance, the inherent value parents place on honesty, recognizing its importance in fostering trust and nurturing relationships. A person of integrity upholds this value as an essential characteristic, demonstrating their commitment to authenticity and moral principles. Similarly, a good leader embraces justice as a core value, striving to create fairness and equity in their actions and decisions.

It's crucial to remember that the core processes of being present, cognitive defusion, and acceptance are not isolated psychotherapy techniques. Instead, they serve as guiding beacons illuminating a path to a more fulfilling and vital life—one that resonates with the values that hold deep significance to you. They serve as guideposts, allowing you to navigate the complexities of life and make choices that are consistent with your personal values.

Embracing your values and integrating them into your daily life is a transformative practice that empowers you to live authentically and with purpose. It's a reminder that your actions can be a reflection of what truly matters to you, guiding you towards a life of greater meaning and fulfillment.

Throughout this process, be gentle with yourself. Recognize that exploring and clarifying your values is a personal and ongoing journey. Allow yourself the freedom to discover what truly resonates within your heart and soul. Embrace the growth and self-discovery that unfolds as you align your actions with your values.

Remember, your values are unique to you and they provide a foundation for living a life that is true to who you are. By embracing these values and integrating them into your daily choices, you can cultivate a sense of purpose and a deep sense of fulfillment. Trust yourself and the wisdom that emerges as you embrace your values and create a life that is meaningful and authentic.

How to Discover Your Personal Core Values

Discovering your personal core values is an empowering journey that allows you to unearth the qualities that truly resonate with your needs, desires, and what genuinely matters to you in life. By delving deep within yourself and exploring your inner landscape, you can uncover profound guiding forces that will illuminate your path and shape your decision-making process. This exploration will enable you to discern what you aspire to embrace and what you wish to avoid in your life's journey.

Through the transformative core process of Acceptance and Commitment Therapy (ACT), you have the opportunity to harness your own moral compass and navigate life in alignment with your personal values. These values act as steadfast guideposts, highlighting the aspects of life that you hold dear. When faced with challenging situations, your personal core values serve as beacons, allowing you to consciously choose behaviors that align with the standards and principles you have set for yourself.

Discovering your personal core values is a deeply personal and introspective process. It involves looking within and listening to the whispers of your heart and soul. Take the time to reflect on what truly matters to you, what brings you joy, and what ignites your passion. Pay attention to moments in your life when you feel most alive and fulfilled, as these can often provide insights into the values that resonate deeply within you.

As you embark on this journey, be patient and kind to yourself. Embrace the fluidity and evolution of your values, knowing that they may shift and transform as you grow and experience life. Allow yourself the freedom to explore and discover new facets of your core values. Remember that your values are unique to you and they represent the essence of who you are.

Be open to the wisdom that emerges as you discover your personal core values. Embrace them as guiding lights that illuminate your path and empower you to live a life that is true to yourself. By aligning your decisions and actions with your core values, you can cultivate a sense of authenticity, purpose, and fulfillment.

Remember, this journey of self-discovery is ongoing. As you continue to explore and deepen your understanding of your personal core values, allow them to evolve and shape your life's direction. Embrace the power within you to choose a life that is rich with meaning, guided by the principles and qualities that resonate at the core of your being.

Embrace the Awareness of Your Emerging Values

Discovering your values requires a mindful and introspective approach. Creating a space of tranquility and solitude is vital in this process, allowing you the opportunity to delve deep within yourself. Find a quiet sanctuary where you can retreat, undisturbed by external distractions.

In this sacred space, you have the freedom to explore your inner landscape and connect with the essence of who you truly are. Take a moment to silence your phone, creating a sanctuary of stillness and tranquility. To enhance your focus and relaxation, consider incorporating calming elements such as soothing music or the gentle aroma of lavender oil, known for its ability to promote a sense of calm and well-being.

As you settle into this serene environment, give yourself permission to be fully present. Cultivate a state of mindfulness, allowing your attention to gently rest on the sensations and thoughts arising within you. Tune in to the whispers of your heart and the wisdom of your soul.

With each mindful breath, bring your awareness to the qualities and traits that resonate deeply within you. What stirs your passion? What brings you a sense of fulfillment and joy? Reflect on the moments in your life when you felt most alive and aligned with your true self. These are the seeds of your emerging values, waiting to be acknowledged and embraced.

As you explore, remember to be gentle and compassionate with yourself. This is an intimate process, and it's natural for values to evolve and unfold over time. Allow yourself the freedom to explore without judgment or expectation. Trust in the wisdom of your inner self to guide you towards the values that truly matter to you.

Embrace this moment of self-discovery as a gift—a chance to align your life with what truly resonates within your soul. By being mindful and conscious of your emerging values, you open the door to a life of greater authenticity, purpose, and fulfillment. Embrace the journey, and let your values be the compass that guides you towards a life that reflects the essence of who you are.

Reconnect with Meaningful Moments in Your Life

Rediscover the moments in your life that hold special significance by taking a moment to reflect on both the times of great happiness and those that brought you deep sadness. These experiences, like signposts along your life's path, offer valuable insights into your personal values.

As you recall these significant moments, pay attention to the intricate details that surround each memory. Allow the emotions and sensations to wash over you, fully immersing yourself in the essence of those moments. Remember, it is not the accolades or external validation that matter here, but rather the moments that shaped you and touched the core of your being.

For instance, perhaps it was the simple joy of your family's first visit to the beach that left an indelible mark on your heart. This memory may not be directly linked to achievements or success, but it holds profound meaning in terms of your personality and the connections you cherish with your loved ones.

As you explore these memories, look for common threads that weave through them. Notice any patterns or themes that emerge. These themes could be influenced by your spiritual beliefs, political leanings, or the values you hold dear. They might be rooted in emotions like anger, sadness, or a deep sense of justice. Take note of these emotional triggers and acknowledge their significance in shaping your values.

In this introspective journey, also be attuned to the aspects that seem absent from your memories. Is there something missing, a void waiting to be filled? Seek to uncover the values that could have been overlooked during moments of joy and happiness. They may reveal hidden treasures that can enrich your life with even greater meaning and fulfillment.

Embrace the depth and complexity of your experiences, for they are the threads that weave together your personal values. By reconnecting with these meaningful moments, you can gain clarity and insight into what truly matters to you. Let your memories serve as guideposts as you embark on a path of aligning your actions and choices with the values that resonate with the essence of who you are.

Understanding the Depth of Human Needs

At the core of our being, we all share essential needs that flow through the fabric of our existence. These needs are intertwined with the very essence of what it means to be human and are deeply connected to the intricate threads of our physical and social existence. By delving into these universal human needs, we can embark on a journey of self-discovery, gaining invaluable insights that can help shape our personal values.

Our values often find their roots in these profound human needs, igniting a deep sense of passion and commitment within us. By delving into the essence of these needs, we can uncover a powerful source of inspiration to guide our lives.

Consider the range of needs that underlie our human experience:

Physical Requirements: Our bodies necessitate sustenance, water, shelter, and clothing to thrive.

Peace: A sense of hope, acceptance, and tranquility allows us to find ease of mind amidst life's challenges.

Connection: The bonds we form with others are nurtured through consideration, respect, and the warmth of genuine connection.

Autonomy: Our individuality seeks expression, dignity, and the freedom to make choices that align with our true selves.

Play: Embracing joy, humor, and adventure enriches our lives, invigorating our spirits with a childlike sense of wonder.

Meaning: Understanding the world around us, participating in something greater than ourselves, and celebrating the moments that define our journey infuse our lives with purpose.

These universal needs form the foundation upon which our personal values take shape. Reflecting on these needs and how they resonate within us can illuminate the values that hold the greatest significance in our lives.

By recognizing the depth of these human needs and their profound influence on our well-being, we can begin to craft a value system that guides us towards a more fulfilled existence. Let these needs serve as gentle reminders of what truly matters, inspiring us to make choices and take actions that honor the essence of our humanity.

Exploring Your Personal Core Values

Begin the process of discovering your personal core values by creating a preliminary list of values that resonate deeply with you. This step involves connecting your own life experiences with the values that hold significance in your culture and, most importantly, to you. Consider both the fundamental needs inherent in our human nature and the values shaped by our biological composition.

As you write down your values, use language that reflects your true self. For instance, if you cherish truth, you might express it as "I embrace the courage of honesty and integrity." This personal touch ensures that your values align authentically with who you are.

Start by jotting down at least seven core values, understanding that the list can be refined further down the line to encompass three central values that truly define you.

Reflecting on the Practice of Your Values

Recognize that personal values can manifest differently from the strategies you employ to embody them. Often, these strategies are influenced by the values instilled by your family. By gaining a deeper understanding of how you put your values into practice, you can gain valuable insights into the driving forces that lead you to engage in actions you can be proud of.

For example, if one of your core values is service, consider the ways in which you choose to live out this value. Will you pursue elected positions to serve your community, or will you dedicate your time to volunteering in a charitable organization? If peace is a value you hold dear, do you actively promote a peaceful environment in your home, or do you take on the role of a peacemaker, facilitating reconciliation among those who hold differing opinions? It is crucial to establish strong connections between your values and the actions you take on a daily basis.

By delving into how you embody your personal values, you gain a deeper understanding of their practical application in your life. This insight allows you to cultivate a greater sense of alignment between your values and your actions, leading to a more meaningful and purpose-driven existence.

Reflecting on the Impact of Your Choices

In this step, it's helpful to consider both hypothetical and real-life situations that require decision-making. Take a moment to contemplate how you would navigate a choice between staying close to your loved ones and pursuing a career opportunity overseas, particularly if your core value is centered around the love of family. Similarly, if independence is a core value for you, think about how you would approach the decision of moving in with your significant other.

These scenarios provide opportunities for your personal values to guide you towards creative decision-making that reflects your care for yourself and those around you. It's important to recognize that the real value of your core values emerges when you face real-life choices. At times, we may become deeply attached to a particular value, assuming it will always lead us to the best decision. However, through mindful consideration of our values, we can gain a clearer understanding of their influence on our decision-making process.

Crafting Your Final List of Personal Core Values

After going through the first six steps, you should now be ready to compile your final list of values that truly resonate with you. Remember, these values should be rooted in your initial inclination towards what is essential to you. Additionally, integrate the insights you gained from articulating your values and examining their impact in different scenarios. Aim to distill your list to three to four primary values that truly embody who you are.

These values serve as powerful tools that can reshape your perspective and guide you towards living the life you genuinely desire. Embracing your personal core values empowers you to make choices that align with your deepest aspirations, paving the way for a more authentic and fulfilling journey.

CHAPTER 3: SETTING GOALS THROUGH ACCEPTANCE AND COMMITMENT THERAPY

A CT: Setting Goals Aligned with Your Values

ACT, with its empathetic approach, recognizes the significance of setting goals that resonate with your personal values. By following these three essential steps, you can embark on a transformative journey of growth and fulfillment:

1. Choose an area of your life to focus on:
   Deliberate on the different aspects of your life, from

community to romance, education to career, personal growth to environment, and beyond. Select an area that deeply resonates with you, where you yearn for progress and positive change.

2. Establish SMART goals:
   Ensure that your goals are Specific, Meaningful, Adaptive, Realistic, and Time-Bound, providing a strong foundation for your aspirations.

Specific: Be precise about the actions you intend to take. Understand the necessary steps involved and break them down into tangible, actionable items. By outlining specific goals, you create a clear path to achievement and can easily assess your progress. For example, instead of setting a vague goal of spending more time with your child, consider aiming for at least one hour of dedicated playtime together each day. Clarity empowers you to track your achievements effectively.

Meaningful: Reflect on whether your goals truly align with your core values or if they are influenced by external pressures or societal expectations. It is crucial to ensure that your goals hold personal significance and contribute to a sense of purpose in your life. Let the guiding light of your core values shape and inspire your goal-setting process.

Adaptive: Continuously evaluate whether your goals are guiding you toward a path that enhances your overall well-being and aligns with your life's purpose. Embrace the flexibility to adapt your goals as you grow and change. Regularly reassess their alignment with your evolving needs and aspirations.

Realistic: Seek a harmonious balance between setting goals that are challenging enough to inspire growth yet attainable within your current circumstances. Goals that are too easy may fail to ignite your passion, while goals that are excessively ambitious can lead to feelings of disappointment or frustration. Be realistic and practical in determining the level of difficulty that resonates with you.

Time-Bound: Infuse your goals with a sense of structure and focus by specifying a time frame or deadline for their achievement. If setting a specific date is not feasible, establish a realistic time frame and commit to working diligently within that period. By incorporating time-bound elements, you foster accountability and ensure progress towards your desired outcomes.

1. **Determine the urgency of your goals**:
   Categorize your goals based on their time horizon to establish a strategic approach to their attainment:

Long-term: Develop a comprehensive plan outlining the actions required to move closer to your goals over the span of six months to one year. Embrace patience and dedication as you work towards achieving these long-term aspirations.

Medium-term: Identify the specific steps you need to take within two to three months to make substantial progress towards your goals. Break down the journey into manageable milestones, allowing for a sense of accomplishment along the way.

Short-term: Create a practical and actionable list of items that can be accomplished within a month. These short-term goals contribute to your overall progress, reinforcing your commitment and motivation.

Immediate: Pinpoint goals that demand your immediate attention, to be achieved within a week or even within a day. Tackling these urgent goals adds momentum to your journey and builds a foundation of consistent action.

By aligning your actions with your personal core values, you ignite a profound passion that propels you towards committed action. Remember, the true essence of our plans and values emerges when supported by purposeful steps. Equipped with a clear understanding of your core values, embark on the transformative journey towards living a truly fulfilling and meaningful life.

CHAPTER 4: HEALING FROM POST-TRAUMATIC STRESS DISORDER: EMPOWERING RECOVERY THROUGH ACCEPTANCE AND COMMITMENT THERAPY

I f you have endured the impact of a shocking, terrifying, or life-threatening event, you may find yourself grappling with a condition known as Post-Traumatic Stress Disorder (PTSD).

These traumatic experiences can range from devastating losses, such as a house fire or the death of a loved one, to surviving harrowing accidents. The intensity of the event, the feelings of horror, helplessness, and the potential for serious injury or death can significantly contribute to the development of PTSD.

Recognizing the Symptoms of PTSD

- *Re-experiencing symptoms:* When someone endures Post-Traumatic Stress Disorder (PTSD), they often find themselves trapped in the haunting grip of reliving the traumatic event within the corridors of their mind. For instance, imagine a person who suffered the devastating loss of their home in a fatal fire that claimed the life of a beloved family member. This individual may encounter distressing flashbacks, vividly replaying the harrowing scenes. Such traumatic events can leave individuals feeling overwhelmed, their sense of power diminished, as they grapple with intrusive thoughts and flashbacks. The resurfacing of these memories drains their energy and makes it challenging to move forward with their day, as they are forced to confront the trauma repeatedly.

- *Avoidance symptoms:* Those affected by PTSD often find themselves engaged in a delicate dance of avoidance, seeking refuge from anything that may trigger memories of their traumatic experience. Consider the case of someone who lost a loved one in a water accident, such as a boat capsizing. The fear of revisiting the tragedy and the haunting anticipation of reliving the horrific event can lead them to actively avoid situations involving boats. In their pursuit of peace, they steer clear of anything that might evoke memories of the traumatic incident, further burdening their emotional well-being.

- **Hyperarousal symptom:** Surviving a traumatic event can sensitize an individual's nervous system, transforming even the most innocuous stimuli into triggers for anxiety and distress. Everyday occurrences such as loud noises or bright lights can suddenly become overwhelming, triggering intense responses rooted in primal survival instincts. In addition, individuals grappling with PTSD may struggle with sleep disturbances and difficulties concentrating, leading to a cascade of challenges that erode happiness and breed bitterness. These heightened reactions can disrupt their overall well-being and hinder their ability to find solace and tranquility.

- **Cognition and mood symptoms:** A frequent manifestation of PTSD is the difficulty in recalling specific details of the traumatic event. The rush of adrenaline experienced during the incident can lead to fragmented or even blocked memories, creating gaps in their recollection. Moreover, individuals may grapple with feelings of guilt, blaming themselves or others for the incident, burdened by the belief that they could have prevented or mitigated the trauma. Such overwhelming guilt can cast a shadow over their sense of self and profoundly impact their emotional landscape. Additionally, PTSD can strip away the joy and interest once found in activities that were once cherished, leaving individuals with a sense of detachment and loss.

Treating PTSD with Compassionate Support

While there are various approaches to treating Post-Traumatic Stress Disorder, one of the most effective methods is Acceptance and Commitment Therapy. In fact, ACT is widely regarded as the most successful form of treatment, with individuals experiencing significant symptom relief in as few as twelve sessions.

ACT offers a compassionate and supportive framework that empowers individuals to confront their traumatic experiences, regain control over their lives, and cultivate resilience. By embracing acceptance, learning valuable coping skills, and committing to meaningful actions aligned with personal values, individuals can gradually overcome the debilitating effects of PTSD.

Remember, seeking support and engaging in therapy can pave the way for healing and the restoration of a fulfilling life, free from the constraints of Post-Traumatic Stress Disorder.

Exploring Treatment Methods for PTSD

When it comes to addressing the symptoms of Post-Traumatic Stress Disorder (PTSD), there are several treatment methods available that strive to alleviate distress and empower individuals to regain control over their lives. Each approach is designed to provide support and guidance tailored to the unique needs of those affected. Let's take a closer look at some commonly used methods:

Prolonged Exposure: Following a traumatic event, it's understandable that individuals would want to avoid anything that triggers distressing memories. However, prolonged exposure therapy offers an alternative approach. By gradually exposing individuals to their traumatic memories over time, this therapy aims to desensitize them and reduce the power these memories hold. Numerous scientific studies have shown that this method can effectively eliminate recurring symptoms, anxiety arousal, and avoidance behaviors associated with PTSD. What's truly remarkable is that positive progress is often observed within just a few therapy sessions, providing a glimmer of hope and much-needed relief.

Cognitive Processing Therapy: Traumatic events can cause individuals to develop maladaptive thought patterns that intensify the impact of their trauma. Cognitive processing therapy creates a safe space for individuals to identify and restructure these distorted thoughts. By finding meaning in the trauma and addressing cognitive distortions, individuals can reduce anxiety and enhance their self-esteem. This therapy has consistently demonstrated high success rates in alleviating PTSD symptoms. However, it's crucial for the individual to actively engage and cooperate throughout the therapeutic process to maximize the potential for positive outcomes.

Seeking Safety: Trauma has a profound impact on a person's emotional regulation, often leading to heightened sensitivity and fear responses. Seeking Safety is an approach specifically designed to help individuals overcome emotional dysregulation and effectively manage their extreme fears. Mindfulness practices are frequently integrated into the therapeutic process, allowing individuals to redirect their attention to the present moment. By doing so, the likelihood of intrusive traumatic memories resurfacing is reduced, enabling individuals to cultivate a sense of safety and stability in their lives.

***Eye Movement Desensitization and Reprocessing
(EMDR):*** EMDR combines elements of exposure therapy with
bilateral stimulation, typically involving eye movements. Although the effectiveness of EMDR has been subject to scrutiny in recent years, some therapists continue to utilize this approach. Similar to prolonged exposure therapy, individuals are
guided through mentally revisiting their traumatic experiences
while engaging in specific eye exercises. The aim is to process
and integrate the traumatic memories in a healthier and more
adaptive manner, ultimately reducing the distress associated
with them.

Research has revealed that attempting to suppress thoughts related to PTSD is often ineffective and can even exacerbate the
frequency of unwanted thoughts and emotions. Additionally,
avoidance and dissociation, which may occur during the initial
trauma, can worsen PTSD symptoms. Acceptance and Commitment Therapy provides a versatile approach that extends
beyond fear-based reactions commonly associated with PTSD.
It can be applied to various diagnoses, comorbidities, and daily
life challenges. ACT addresses a wide range of responses and
focuses on promoting self-examination, acceptance, and commitment to behavior change. By doing so, it aims to enhance
the quality of life for individuals living with PTSD and other
mental health conditions.

Acceptance and Commitment Therapy incorporates three essential components into its protocol, fostering a collaborative process between the therapist and the client:

Generation of Values Narratives: As part of the therapy process, clients are encouraged to reflect on their values and priorities in various areas of life, such as family, intimate relationships, employment, health, and spirituality. This self-reflection may involve completing assignments or exercises outside of therapy sessions. Clients describe their values and priorities, which are then carefully reviewed and refined together with the therapist. This collaborative exploration helps individuals gain a deeper understanding of what truly matters to them.

Rating of Values Narratives: Once values are identified, clients are prompted to rate them in absolute terms, considering their personal significance. Additionally, clients assess how successfully they believe they have lived up to these values in their lives thus far. This self-evaluation provides valuable insight into the alignment between their values and their actions. Furthermore, clients are encouraged to rank their values in order of importance, establishing a clearer hierarchy to guide decision-making and goal setting.

Identification of Goals, Actions, and Barriers: In this phase, clients identify specific goals they wish to achieve based on their values and priorities. Together with the therapist, they outline concrete actions required to work towards these goals. Additionally, clients identify potential obstacles or barriers that may hinder their progress. Through open and honest discussion, the therapist and client explore strategies to overcome these barriers. The therapist remains steadfast in motivating the client to persevere despite any challenges that may arise, fostering resilience and determination.

Throughout the ACT process, the therapist provides unwavering support, understanding, and encouragement. The focus is on empowering the client to take meaningful steps towards their goals, aligning their actions with their deeply held values. By embracing acceptance, exploring personal values, and committing to positive change, individuals can cultivate a more fulfilling and purpose-driven life. The therapist and client work together as partners on this journey, nurturing growth, and facilitating the client's progress towards a more authentic and valued existence.

CHAPTER 5: HARNESSING ACCEPTANCE AND COMMITMENT THERAPY TO NAVIGATE DEPRESSION

F rom the perspective of Acceptance and Commitment Therapy, depression is seen as a manifestation of avoidance behavior and psychological inflexibility. It encompasses a range of behaviors, thoughts, and emotions that are interconnected with one's way of functioning. These depressive behaviors often serve as a strategy to avoid personal experiences and can be particularly challenging for individuals with Borderline Personality Disorder and related mood/emotional disorders. However, there is hope for change and growth.

Developing effective skills to manage depression is crucial, and it starts with understanding that your reactions to situations are influenced by learned behaviors and your environment. By relearning how to process and navigate emotions, you can gradually rebuild your ability to tolerate distress.

ACT places a strong emphasis on developing the capacity to handle distressing situations, whether they stem from past trauma, current circumstances, or general worries. In many cases, individuals may struggle to rationalize why certain things happen to them or why they experience certain emotions. Unlike some other therapeutic approaches that focus on problem-solving and proactive change, ACT emphasizes acceptance.

The reason behind this emphasis on acceptance is that individuals who could benefit from ACT often tend to overcompensate when they try to assert control over their problems. They may experience emotional overreactions or other difficulties in response to various triggers. This differs from the typical response to overwhelming stimuli, which is often confusion and stagnation until a clear path forward is identified.

Therefore, ACT places great importance on not allowing stressful stimuli to heavily impact one's emotional well-being. It involves learning to let these stimuli affect you less, maintaining a sense of inner calm amid external challenges.

Developing the ability to navigate stressful conditions is vital for leading a happy and healthy life. Without effective strategies for dealing with emotional trauma and general distress, sustained happiness can be elusive. Chances are, you are pursuing this course because you struggle with managing your emotions as they arise.

It's essential to recognize that attempting to block out or change situations that are beyond your control often has little effect. Accepting this reality is not a sign of giving up; on the contrary, rejecting it is what prevents growth because it means you are not willing to face the challenges in front of you.

Often, people develop a mentality of self-rejection as a response to various triggers. Recognizing the causes of this self-rejection and finding ways to avoid those triggers is an important part of Dialectical Behavior Therapy.

ACT provides various methods and techniques that can help you practice and develop skills to manage depression effectively. Consistent practice in your daily life is crucial so that you can internalize these skills and apply them intuitively when needed. Remember, change takes time and effort, but with commitment and practice, you can cultivate a greater sense of well-being and resilience.

It's important to review these strategies daily, especially during times when you feel trapped in the grip of depression. This repetition will help solidify them in your mind. Consider finding a way to carry these strategies with you, whether it's through note cards or a mobile app, so you can easily access them when needed.

The first set of strategies focuses on distraction. When faced with distressing emotions or situations, the goal is to divert your attention in a productive manner. This ties in with your mindfulness practice, as developing your ability to focus will enable you to shift your attention quickly and manage internal struggles effectively. These distraction techniques are part of building emotional resilience and tolerance for challenging situations.

Another important aspect to focus on is self-soothing. This concept is emphasized in Dialectical Behavior Therapy. Self-soothing involves finding ways to be kind and comforting to yourself. It's crucial to remember that you shouldn't be constantly running without giving yourself opportunities to release stress. Allowing periods of leisure and simplicity helps you decompress and unload. Taking this time is essential because it allows your mind to reset and create a fresh starting point.

Many individuals with ongoing emotional issues find that high-stress environments and a lack of opportunities for decompression can exacerbate their problems. While this won't solve all your emotional challenges at once, it can certainly help you process them more effectively when you're out and about. Recognizing that you have the chance to destress later in the day can make it easier to navigate daily stressors. Don't hesitate to set aside dedicated time for yourself.

During this personal time, the activities you choose are entirely up to you. There's no right or wrong choice. Similar to the final rule of meditation, the goal is to be effective by doing what works for you. Discover the activities that soothe and relax you. It could be taking a bath in the evening, reading literature in your favorite genre, or engaging in a hobby or project. The key is to be kind to yourself and allow yourself the opportunity to unwind. Remember, there's nothing wrong with taking time for yourself. Incorporate this important aspect into your daily routine during the depression block.

Now, let's take a moment to address a serious matter. It's true that many people who practice Acceptance and Commitment Therapy do so because they have Borderline Personality Disorder. The prognosis for individuals with this disorder can be challenging. While therapy and possibly medication can help treat it, it's important to acknowledge that approximately ten percent of individuals with Borderline Personality Disorder may ultimately take their own lives. This is a deeply tragic and alarming statistic.

If you're reading this because you suspect you have Borderline Personality Disorder or have already been diagnosed, I strongly urge you to seek the assistance of a medical professional who can provide in-person support and guide you through various treatment options. Depression is a real and heavy burden, and it often coexists with Borderline Personality Disorder. While everyone can benefit from the skills developed through Dialectical Behavior Therapy, if you're here because you suspect you have Borderline Personality Disorder, it's crucial to seek professional help and find a program with a personal therapist who can provide you with the best and most tailored support possible.

I want to acknowledge that encouraging yourself can be incredibly challenging, especially if you're dealing with depression alongside your mood or personality disorder. It's not as simple as just telling yourself that you can do anything because, in reality, it's unlikely that you'll immediately believe it. You might find yourself questioning your abilities and feeling uncertain about the idea of cheering yourself on. This starting point can feel disheartening, but it's important to persist and fake it until you make it.

There are several reasons why this approach can be helpful. Your brain has a remarkable capacity to accept what it's repeatedly exposed to. By consistently telling yourself that you can do something, your brain will gradually begin to believe it. The words and actions you choose have a significant impact on your emotional well-being, and recent psychological studies have demonstrated the real effects of the "fake it until you make it" phenomenon on your brain's structure.

Furthermore, the act of affirming to yourself that you can handle challenges and accept whatever comes your way is incredibly powerful. It's like wielding a psychological sword. By doing this, you develop the skill of acceptance and the ability to navigate through any situation, regardless of its difficulty. Affirming to yourself that you can do it holds weight and influence.

Over time, you will cultivate a genuine belief in yourself because you will continually overcome the obstacles you face. Even if you currently struggle to believe it, remember that you have the capacity to cope with whatever comes your way. Consider this: life follows a pattern of either moving forward or reaching rock bottom, which implies a state of dying. If you're not dying, you're still progressing. Find security in this fact. Your mind is designed to handle various challenges, even if it takes time. It may have become accustomed to dealing with things in an unhealthy manner, but that doesn't mean you can't change that.

It's essential to acknowledge that difficult things are indeed hard. You will need to put in effort to overcome them, as that's the nature of facing challenges. However, if you keep this in mind and work on accepting this reality, you will gradually realize that when you tell yourself you can handle something, you truly can. This reinforcement strengthens your statement and builds your resilience.

Moreover, constantly reminding yourself that you can handle whatever comes your way makes you more prepared and resilient for future difficulties. If things do get worse or if another setback occurs, you'll remember that you have the capacity to navigate through them. You possess the power to make things happen, no matter what it takes. This self-encouragement is your most potent tool.

With that, we conclude the specific set of strategies for improvement. As mentioned earlier, try to incorporate these into your daily routine during the depression block, so they become more ingrained in your memory. Consider finding a way to have them readily accessible when you need them the most. You could write them down in a notes app on your phone, summarize them for easy reference, or even take screenshots if you're reading this on a device like a Kindle or a Books app.

The next important aspect of dealing with depression is the ability to evaluate the pros and cons of a situation. Take a moment to reflect on your current circumstances and consider the potential positives and negatives that could arise if you choose not to tolerate the situation. Is there an opportunity for real and proactive change that you can initiate?

Often, when you actively try not to do something, your mind may respond with a kickback reaction that persists until you address it. It's crucial to respond to this response, unless it is a compulsion related to OCD, in which case it's best to avoid meditating on it. Take the time to realistically analyze what would happen if you were to respond to the situation and objectively weigh the potential outcomes. While it's not ideal to indulge in this habit frequently, it can be helpful to objectively consider the consequences in situations where you experience a kickback response.

Another skill to practice is the concept of total acceptance. Many times, we find ourselves actively resisting the reality of a situation. This resistance can stem from a sense of being unable to handle it or a fear of losing control. In such instances, it's important to allow yourself to fully and completely accept whatever is happening to you.

The truth is, you cannot change a reality that is beyond your control, no matter how hard you try. Focusing on your inability to change it will only lead to frustration. There are certain things in life that you have limited influence over, and in these cases, you can only do what is within your power. No amount of action will alter the outcome.

For example, consider a situation where a family member is dealing with an illness. What can you realistically do to change this stressful circumstance? Can you cure their illness or fight against it? Unfortunately, the answer is no. It's painful, but the only healthy approach is to accept that you cannot change what may happen.

Practicing this acceptance goes hand in hand with your mindfulness strategies and willpower, enabling you to develop another essential skill: turning your mind around. The goal of this skill is to enhance your ability to accept what is happening rather than rejecting it. In conditions like Borderline Personality Disorder, one of the major challenges is developing a tendency to resist whatever is occurring. The knee-jerk reaction is often to reject the situation because it feels like losing control or becoming powerless.

It's important for you to work on honing the skill of acceptance so that you can start embracing whatever may happen in your life. Practicing the ability to make yourself accept things is a valuable habit to cultivate. While it's not necessary to accept everything that comes your way, it's crucial to learn to accept those things that are beyond your control. Reacting in any other way would be irrational, considering there was little you could have done to change the outcome. It's natural to debate and question the meaning of acceptance and whether you have the power to change certain things, but often the simplest answer is that you can't.

By building the habit of acceptance, you will gradually shift towards a healthier state of mind that allows you to engage with things and concepts in a more constructive way. You will become more adept at processing your emotions.

All of these skills culminate in the final skill of dealing with depression, which is distinguishing between being willing to take action and being excessively willful. Willingness involves the desire to take action that can genuinely have an impact. For instance, if you're unhappy with your income and have the financial means to pursue further education, you should be willing to do so. It's important not to settle for a subpar situation in life just because you've developed an acceptance mindset. On the other hand, willfulness refers to the urge to change things that are beyond your control. Excessive willfulness creates inner tension and undermines your ability to accept what cannot be changed. You must release that tension and allow yourself to accept those aspects of life that are beyond your influence. By doing so, you will discover a greater sense of happiness and develop a healthier perspective on life. You'll no longer obsess over changing things you cannot control, but you'll find yourself more willing to take effective action.

With that, we conclude the chapter on depression. It's important to practice all these skills during your designated depression block. However, it's equally crucial to carry these skills into your daily life beyond the designated block. The block provides a focused time for training and retention of these methods, but their true value lies in how you incorporate them into your day-to-day experiences.

If you're considering implementing all of these techniques at once, I urge caution. It's more effective to take a gradual approach in your therapy. Your brain is not accustomed to handling such rapid change. Remember, this journey is a marathon, not a sprint, as I mentioned earlier. Your success with these methods depends on your ability to retain and actively apply them. Keep them with you, but avoid overwhelming yourself by trying to tackle everything at once.

Studies suggest that ACT may be more effective in one-on-one therapy sessions rather than group sessions. Additionally, research shows that ACT can be particularly beneficial in treating certain conditions, including depression, especially in reducing self-harm behaviors among individuals with depression.

CHAPTER 6: MASTERING ANXIETY THROUGH ACCEPTANCE AND COMMITMENT THERAPY

L iving with anxiety can be a challenging experience, especially when intrusive thoughts disrupt our daily lives. These thoughts, influenced by the nature of our anxiety, can vary depending on the specific type of anxiety we face. It's important to recognize that each individual's struggle with anxiety is unique, and understanding the different forms it can take can help us navigate our journey towards healing and relief.

Generalized anxiety disorder often brings intrusive thoughts about our loved ones, causing us to worry excessively about their well-being. On the other hand, individuals with social anxiety disorder may constantly battle thoughts that remind them of embarrassing moments, intensifying their fear of judgment in social situations. These are just a couple of examples among the wide range of anxiety disorders, including social anxiety disorder, agoraphobia, selective mutism, separation anxiety, panic disorder, and specific phobias.

It is estimated that approximately 12 percent of the population experiences an anxiety disorder within a given year, while the lifetime prevalence rate ranges from five to 30 percent. Typically, anxiety disorders tend to manifest between the ages of 15 and 35, impacting individuals during crucial stages of personal and professional development. Among the various anxiety disorders, phobias are the most common, affecting numerous individuals worldwide.

Anxiety disorders can arise from a combination of genetic predispositions and environmental factors. Traumatic experiences, such as childhood abuse or growing up in challenging conditions like poverty, can contribute to the development of anxiety disorders later in life. Furthermore, individuals with anxiety disorders often face additional mental health conditions, including depression and personality disorders. The cumulative burden of living with an anxiety disorder, whether it exists on its own or alongside other disorders, can take a toll on our overall well-being and increase the risk of physical health complications such as heart disease, substance abuse, or hyperthyroidism.

Thankfully, effective treatment options are available for managing anxiety disorders. Cognitive Behavioral Therapy, combined with appropriate pharmaceutical interventions when necessary, forms the cornerstone of treatment. Additionally, mindfulness exercises have proven to be beneficial in reducing anxiety symptoms and promoting a sense of calm and clarity. For individuals with obsessive-compulsive disorder self-help resources can play a valuable role in their journey towards managing their symptoms and regaining control over their lives.

Remember, you are not alone in your struggle with anxiety. With the right support, understanding, and treatment, it is possible to navigate the challenges posed by anxiety and find a path towards a more fulfilling and peaceful life.

Understanding Your Anxiety: Exploring the Depths of Fear

Anxiety has a way of infiltrating your thoughts and casting a shadow of uncertainty over your future. When anxiety takes hold, it can have a profound impact on your overall well-being and quality of life. Its weight can distort your perception, causing you to perceive problems where none exist. This perpetual state of unease can push you to extremes, leading to social withdrawal or even aggressive behavior, which in turn hinders your ability to connect with others and find a sense of belonging.

Fear, both in the mind and body, manifests itself in a multitude of ways, leaving a profound impact on your holistic well-being. When fear or anxiety takes hold, your body and mind operate in overdrive, triggering a cascade of physical and psychological responses. These responses can include an accelerated heartbeat, rapid breathing, weakened muscles, profuse sweating, stomach pains, difficulty concentrating, lightheadedness, a feeling of being paralyzed, loss of appetite, hot and cold sweats, tense muscles, and a dry mouth.

Experiencing these physical symptoms of fear can be incredibly frustrating, especially when the underlying cause of your fear or anxiety remains unclear. Fear can be triggered by a myriad of factors, and sometimes our brains continue to send distress signals unnecessarily. However, by cultivating self-awareness, you can enhance your understanding of your unique relationship with fear and begin to regain a sense of control.

It's important to remember that you are not defined by your anxiety. Acknowledge and explore your fears with compassion and curiosity, allowing yourself the opportunity for growth and healing. As you embark on this journey of self-discovery, it's essential to be patient and kind to yourself, knowing that understanding and managing anxiety takes time and effort. Together, we can navigate the depths of fear, unravel its mysteries, and forge a path towards a more balanced and fulfilling life. You are not alone in this journey, and support is available every step of the way.

Panic Attacks

Experiencing overwhelming mental and physical sensations of fear can be incredibly distressing. Individuals who have had panic attacks often describe difficulty breathing, an increased heartbeat, and a sense of losing control, akin to a heart attack.

Worry

Worrying takes hold when our concerns and fears are magnified, leading us to believe that the future is bleak. It's a state where hope feels lost, and the anticipation of negative events becomes all-consuming.

There are various techniques that can help alleviate fear, worry, anxiety, depression, and other mental disorders:

Face Your Fears

Although it may seem counterintuitive, facing your fears is a powerful approach. By exposing yourself to what you fear, you gain valuable knowledge and insights, enabling you to overcome anxiety more effectively. Through this process, ignorance gives way to understanding, empowering you on your journey to conquer your fears.

Know Yourself

To free yourself from the grip of fear, it is essential to take the time to understand who you truly are. Explore the origins of your fears and reflect on your childhood experiences. Recognize that many of our attitudes and fears are shaped during our early years. By unraveling as much as you can about yourself, you can gain a deeper understanding of your fears and begin to heal.

Exercise

Engaging in physical exercise demands your full attention, diverting your mind from fear and redirecting it to the present moment. Exercise not only helps alleviate fears and anxieties but also improves heart health, enhances blood circulation, strengthens immunity, and effectively reduces negative emotions.

Relax

When you allow your body and mind to relax, fears begin to fade away. Deep breathing exercises, such as adopting a meditation posture and focusing on your breath while clearing your mind of distractions, can induce a state of relaxation and restore balance to your body and mind.

Healthy Eating

Maintaining a clean and nutritious diet is vital for your mental and emotional well-being. A healthy diet focuses on essential nutrients while minimizing the consumption of unhealthy junk foods. Keeping your blood sugar levels stable is crucial, as fluctuating blood sugar can trigger panic attacks and anxiety.

Drink Alcohol in Moderation or Avoid It Altogether

While it may be tempting to turn to alcohol as a temporary escape from nervousness, it's important to recognize that the relief it provides is short-lived. Drinking alcohol is not a sustainable solution for finding calmness. Instead, facing your fears and anxieties with a clear mind and sobriety yields more fruitful results.

Faith

If you believe in a higher power or supernatural entity that watches over the universe and its inhabitants, placing your trust in that faith can be comforting. The more faith you have in this entity, the greater your chances of finding solace and overcoming your fears and anxieties.

Medication

Medications can be a helpful tool, particularly for individuals with time constraints. While they may not be the sole treatment model, when used in conjunction with other therapeutic approaches, medication can provide significant support and relief.

Support Groups

You are not alone in your battle against fears and anxieties. The internet offers a wealth of resources to connect with like-minded individuals who are also navigating similar challenges. Support groups, forums, Facebook communities, and websites are readily available platforms. Before joining a support group, take the time to understand their principles and values, ensuring they align with your needs and preferences.

CHAPTER 7: MANAGING AGGRESSIVE BEHAVIOR WITH ACCEPTANCE AND COMMITMENT THERAPY

A ggressive behavior can take various forms, ranging from less severe acts like grabbing, pushing, and slapping to more serious incidents involving forcible restraint or punching. While research suggests that males are more likely to commit severe acts of aggression, both men and women engage in the more common forms of aggressive behavior. It is crucial to approach this topic with empathy and understanding, recognizing that aggression can affect individuals regardless of gender.

Despite extensive research on aggression and its underlying causes, effective treatment options remain limited. Many existing treatments are outdated and lack robust empirical support. However, through the lens of contextual behavioral science, valuable insights have been gained, leading to the development of a comprehensive model that seeks to address aggression. This model acknowledges that both psychological and physical aggression often serve as means to escape or avoid distressing personal experiences. By examining the underlying processes and incorporating connected techniques and components, a more holistic and effective treatment approach can be achieved.

It is important to recognize the interconnectedness between physical aggression and other mental health concerns such as depression, anxiety, substance use, and physical health issues. Additionally, aggression often contributes to relationship distress, separation, and divorce. Its negative impact extends beyond individual well-being, affecting occupational and cognitive functioning as well. By addressing aggression and its associated challenges, we can work towards alleviating the burden of depression, enhancing relationship management, and fostering overall personal growth.

In this chapter, we will explore compassionate and evidence-based strategies for managing aggressive behavior. By delving into the underlying factors and employing effective interventions, we can empower individuals to transform their lives, promoting healthier relationships, improved mental well-being, and enhanced overall functioning. Together, let us embark on a journey of understanding, healing, and positive change.

In Zarling's enlightening thesis (2013, 6-9), she categorizes the risk factors for aggression, providing us with a deeper understanding of the intricate web of influences that contribute to this complex issue. By exploring these factors with empathy and compassion, we can shed light on the underlying causes and work towards effective interventions and prevention strategies.

- Family - Within the family context, it becomes evident that partner aggression often arises in situations characterized by severe discipline, low cohesion, and acute conflict. These dynamics not only impact the individuals directly involved but also have far-reaching effects on the overall well-being of the family unit. Recognizing the importance of nurturing healthy relationships among non-aggressive adults within the family is crucial for breaking the cycle of aggression.

- Relationship - Aggression can be a precursor to relationship dissolution and distress. It is essential to acknowledge the complexities that arise in intimate relationships and understand that interpersonal skill deficits can amplify the potential for conflict. By addressing these deficits and providing support in building healthy communication and conflict resolution skills, we can create a foundation for more harmonious and fulfilling partnerships.

- Personality and psychopathy - Personality traits and psychopathy emerge as significant predictors of aggression, often rooted in childhood or adolescent antisocial behavior, trauma, or abuse. It is important to approach these factors with empathy and understanding, recognizing that individuals who exhibit aggressive tendencies may have experienced significant challenges in their early lives. By addressing the underlying issues such as depression, trauma, and maladaptive attachment patterns linked to anxiety, we can help individuals develop healthier coping mechanisms and build a more stable sense of self.

- Cognitive and affective factors - Anger, as the most researched factor, plays a pivotal role in aggression. However, it is crucial to explore how individuals respond to anger and understand the underlying cognitive and affective processes. Fear, shame, jealousy, and symptoms reported by individuals experiencing panic attacks may also contribute to aggressive behavior. Approaching these factors with empathy can lead to a deeper understanding of the individual's internal struggles and pave the way for tailored interventions that address their unique needs.

- Other factors - Substance abuse, stress, and relationship characteristics are additional factors that intertwine with aggression. While the exact mechanisms linking these factors to aggression may not be fully understood, it is essential to approach them with compassion and openness. Recognizing the potential impact of verbal aggression and arguments, we can create supportive environments that promote healthier forms of communication and conflict resolution.

In our quest to comprehend the complexity of aggression, it is crucial to approach the subject with empathy and compassion. By expanding our understanding of the multifaceted influences at play, we can develop comprehensive strategies that address the root causes of aggression, promote emotional well-being, and foster healthier relationships. Together, let us strive to create a society built on empathy, understanding, and a shared commitment to reducing aggression and its devastating effects.

By embracing a collaborative and empowering approach like ACT, individuals undergoing treatment for partner aggression can gain the tools and insights necessary to foster lasting change. Understanding the intricacies of aggression and tailoring interventions to address its underlying causes will help us build a future where healthier relationships and non-violent behaviors prevail.

Zarling proposes a therapeutic model that focuses on altering the underlying contexts connected to thoughts and emotions (ibid.). A crucial principle of a more effective model is recognizing the role of avoidance and the influence of fear. Within Acceptance and Commitment Therapy, experiential avoidance is seen as a common link to various forms of anxiety and negative emotional states. Individuals often try to escape internal experiences they find uncomfortable, striving to control or modify these internal processes. They engage in a battle against their own thoughts and feelings. While this coping mechanism may provide short-term relief, it proves inadequate as a long-term strategy for navigating the complexities of daily life and relationships, where challenges are bound to arise. Prolonged thought suppression and rigid thought control are examples of such patterns (Zarling, 2013, 30).

Substance use is another problematic behavior pattern that hinders healthy functioning. Engaging in such behaviors obstructs the development of more adaptive and effective responses. In order to confront these troublesome internal experiences and guide behavior toward actions aligned with personal values, the implementation of acceptance and redirection of values becomes essential. Clinical testing has shown these two processes to be effective in fostering positive change.

Zarling's functional perspective on partner aggression provides a valuable framework for identifying the underlying processes and aligning them with therapeutic interventions (2013, 36). This approach emphasizes practical outcomes, aiming to address the complex nature of aggression.

Differing from feminist perspectives that view aggression as an attempt to overpower women, and contrasting with cognitive-behavioral therapy approaches that attribute aggression directly to anger, Zarling's model presents a distinct understanding. According to ACT, aggression is seen as an efficient strategy to avoid unwanted emotions. Zarling's model recognizes that aggression is triggered by emotional responses and ideas stemming from evocative interpersonal conflicts and past learning experiences (ibid.).

Individuals who engage in partner aggression often retain fear or heightened sensitivity towards their own inner experiences, compelling them to evade these emotions. Such arousal may be more intense among individuals who commit partner aggression, and they may struggle with social interactions, lacking tolerance and skills in this domain (Zarling, 2013, 41 and 42).

This context sets the stage for engaging in aggressive behaviors, which momentarily distract or alleviate the psychological turmoil. The fleeting success of aggression in temporarily averting the unwanted inner experiences reinforces the inclination towards aggressive responses.

By understanding the complex dynamics underlying partner aggression and acknowledging the role of avoidance and fear, individuals can embark on a transformative journey. Embracing therapeutic models like ACT allows individuals to confront their inner experiences, develop healthier coping mechanisms, and align their actions with personal values. Together, we can empower individuals to break free from the cycle of aggression, fostering compassion, understanding, and healthier relationships.

Zarling's model sheds light on the intricate process that gives rise to partner aggression (2013, 38):

STIMULUS (interpersonal conflict) >> INTERNAL EXPERIENCE >> AGGRESSION >> RELIEF

Within this framework, Acceptance and Commitment Therapy emerges as a beacon of hope, offering individuals the opportunity to break free from the chains of aggression and cultivate healthier patterns of behavior. The therapeutic journey aims to dismantle the emotional responses that fuel aggression, opening doors to a more fulfilling and compassionate existence (Zarling, 2013, 46).

By reducing the overwhelming need to control and suppress their inner experiences, individuals can gradually diminish the frequency of aggressive behavior. In the therapeutic space, they are encouraged to gain a deeper understanding of the impact of their aggressive strategies. With the guidance of a compassionate therapist, they begin to unveil the patterns of avoidance and control that have perpetuated their harmful actions.

Through this newfound awareness, individuals embark on a transformative process of unlearning the rigid rules and limitations associated with their previous coping mechanisms. Instead, they are empowered to explore and adopt more adaptive responses to conflicts and triggers. The therapist helps them redirect their behavior towards value-oriented goals, aligning their actions with what truly matters to them.

The exploration of personal values takes center stage in the treatment of partner aggression. Through open and empathetic discussions, individuals delve into the core principles and beliefs that define their authentic selves. This introspective work enables them to construct a new direction, one that is rooted in respect, empathy, and non-violence. By embracing their values, individuals can begin to rebuild their lives on a foundation of healthier relationships and positive engagement.

Mindfulness, a powerful tool integrated into various cognitive-behavioral approaches, plays a vital role in this transformative journey. By cultivating present-moment awareness and non-judgmental acceptance, individuals learn to challenge distorted thought processes and navigate the discomfort that arises within them. Mindfulness serves as a guiding light, illuminating the path towards inner peace and emotional well-being.

As individuals actively engage in the therapeutic process, supported by their compassionate therapist, they embark on a profound journey of personal growth and self-discovery. With each step forward, they gain the tools and insights necessary to break free from the cycle of partner aggression. By embracing empathy, compassion, and emotional well-being, individuals can rewrite their stories, fostering healthier relationships and nurturing a brighter future for themselves and those they love.

CHAPTER 8: LIBERATING YOUR MIND FROM INTRUSIVE AND OBSESSIVE THOUGHTS

L iving with Obsessive Compulsive Disorder (OCD) can be an incredibly challenging experience, especially when plagued by intrusive thoughts. These intrusive thoughts can cause distress and lead to negative self-evaluations, as individuals may believe something is inherently wrong with them for having such thoughts. The constant battle to rid themselves of these intrusive thoughts often leaves individuals feeling trapped in a worsening state.

When it comes to treating OCD, Cognitive Behavioral Therapies are widely recommended, with Acceptance and Commitment Therapy being one approach. According to the Medline
Plus Medical Dictionary, OCD is characterized by unwanted
compulsive thoughts, sensations, emotions, concepts, and behaviors. For individuals with OCD, these sensations become
obsessions that significantly impact their daily lives.

While it's normal to double-check that a door is locked from
time to time, individuals with obsessive tendencies find themselves endlessly and tirelessly checking to ensure the door is truly
secured. The overwhelming nature of obsessive thoughts and
compulsive actions can disrupt a person's normal routines and
leave them feeling helpless in the face of these thoughts.

OCD manifests as a condition where uncontrollable thoughts
and repetitive behaviors take hold. Despite recognizing the ir-
rationality of their thoughts and behaviors, individuals with
OCD struggle to resist the urge to engage in these repetitive
patterns. It can feel like an ongoing battle, causing immense
distress and frustration.

**Within the realm of Obsessive Compulsive Disorder, in-
dividuals can fall into different categories, each with their
unique struggles:**

- *Washers:* These individuals have an intense fear of

contamination by germs, leading to compulsive cleaning rituals in an attempt to alleviate their anxiety. They may spend hours each day engaging in excessive hand-washing, cleaning household items, or avoiding situations they perceive as dirty or contaminated. The constant fear of germs and the need for cleanliness can consume their thoughts and significantly impact their daily lives.

- **Checkers:** People in this category feel compelled to repeatedly check things associated with potential danger or harm, such as locked doors, appliances, or personal belongings. The fear of something going wrong or an accident occurring drives them to perform these checking rituals, often causing distress and consuming a significant amount of their time and energy. Despite realizing that their fears may be irrational, they struggle to resist the urge to check repeatedly, fearing the consequences of not doing so.

- **Doubters and sinners:** This group experiences overwhelming anxiety and fear that if things are not done perfectly or if they engage in morally "wrong" actions, something terrible will occur. They may constantly doubt their decisions, seek reassurance from others, or engage in repetitive behaviors to prevent perceived negative outcomes. The fear of making mistakes or being responsible for negative consequences can lead to significant distress and a sense of being trapped in a cycle of doubt and guilt.

- **Counters and arrangers:** Individuals with these obsessions are preoccupied with order and symmetry. They feel compelled to count objects or arrange them in specific ways to alleviate their distress. Deviations from their preferred patterns can cause immense anxiety, leading them to repeat these actions until they feel a sense of "rightness" or balance. The need for order and symmetry can be all-consuming and can interfere with their ability to focus on other aspects of life.

- **Hoarders:** This category includes individuals who are afraid of discarding possessions, fearing that something terrible might happen if they let go of even the most insignificant items. They struggle with excessive attachment to objects and experience extreme anxiety at the thought of parting with them. As a result, their living spaces become cluttered and disorganized, making it challenging to navigate their environment. The fear of losing something valuable or the belief that items have inherent meaning drives their hoarding behaviors.

No matter which category of OCD you identify with, it's crucial to recognize that your struggles are valid and that help is available. Overcoming OCD can be a challenging journey, but there are numerous techniques, therapies, and support systems that can assist you in finding relief and reclaiming control over your life. Seeking professional help from a qualified mental health provider who specializes in OCD treatment is a vital step in developing a personalized plan to manage your symptoms.

Embracing Your Fears

Facing your fears may feel daunting, but it is an essential step in overcoming Obsessive Compulsive Disorder. While it may seem easier to avoid or shun your fears, this approach can inadvertently strengthen your obsessive patterns and deepen your fears. Instead, consider confronting your triggers head-on and gradually building up your tolerance to them. It won't be easy at first, but by resisting the urge to engage in rituals and reducing the intensity of your rituals over time, you can diminish the power your triggers hold over you. Remember, it's a journey, and every small step towards facing your fears is a step towards regaining control over your thoughts.

Anticipate and Address OCD Urges

Understanding the situations that tend to trigger your OCD is an important part of managing the disorder. By becoming aware of these triggers, you can take proactive steps to address them. For example, if you find yourself obsessively checking whether the doors are locked, try slowing down and taking your time to ensure they are securely locked. Rather than rushing away, create a vivid mental image of the locked door and reassure yourself by labeling it as "The door is locked." By doing so, you provide yourself with a sense of certainty and diminish the compulsion to repeatedly check. When the urge arises, simply bring to mind the image you created and remind yourself that it is just an "obsessive thought," gradually reducing its power over you.

Shift Your Focus

When OCD compulsions arise, it's important to redirect your attention to other activities or interests. Engage in physical exercise, go for a jog, immerse yourself in a captivating book or movie, spend quality time with a supportive friend, or listen to soothing music. The goal is to shift your focus away from the compulsive thought and onto something more positive and engaging. By refocusing your attention for at least fifteen minutes, you can create distance from the compulsive thought and delay your response to it. Over time, you may find that the intensity of the urge diminishes or even disappears entirely, giving you a sense of control over your own mind.

Document Your Compulsive Thoughts

Obsessive thoughts can be overwhelming and persistent, often leading to compulsive behaviors. To gain a better understanding of your thought patterns, consider keeping a record of your obsessive thoughts as they arise. Whether using pen and paper or a digital device, jot down each obsessive thought that enters your mind. This practice can help you observe the frequency and nature of your thoughts, providing valuable insights for therapy and self-reflection. By documenting your compulsive thoughts, you create an opportunity to examine them objectively and gain a deeper understanding of their patterns and triggers, empowering you to develop strategies for managing them effectively.

Allocate Time for OCD Worry

Instead of constantly battling against your compulsions and thoughts, try allocating specific times for worrying. Set aside two dedicated sessions during the day when you can allow yourself to focus on your concerns. However, make sure to choose a time when you are less vulnerable to anxiety. When obsessive thoughts arise outside of your designated worry time, jot them down to revisit during your designated sessions. By doing so, you acknowledge the thoughts without letting them consume your entire day. This approach helps create a structured framework for addressing your worries while ensuring that they do not overwhelm your daily life.

Record Your OCD Obsessions

Consider utilizing a recording device to capture your obsessive thoughts in a structured manner. Select a specific obsession and record yourself explaining the thoughts and fears associated with it in detail. By repeatedly listening to or watching these recordings, you expose yourself to your obsessions in a controlled way. Over time, this exposure can desensitize you to the thoughts and reduce their impact and influence over your daily life. By confronting your obsessions through recorded sessions, you empower yourself to gradually detach from their hold, allowing you to regain control and diminish their power.

Avoid Alcohol and Nicotine

While alcohol may temporarily reduce anxiety and worry, its effects are short-lived. As the alcohol wears off, anxiety can intensify even more. Similarly, cigarettes have been found to increase anxiety levels. Indulging in these substances can perpetuate negative thought cycles and exacerbate the challenges of OCD. Instead, it is beneficial to confront your OCD with a clear and sober mind, allowing you to approach it with greater clarity and resilience.

Spend Quality Time with Friends and Family

Obsessive thoughts can be isolating and overwhelming, leading to a sense of detachment from the world around you. However, isolating yourself only strengthens the grip of OCD on your life. By prioritizing connections with your loved ones, you can find grounding and support. Engaging in activities and meaningful conversations with friends and family can help divert your attention away from your obsessive thoughts and remind you of the joy and fulfillment that exist beyond the realm of OCD. Building a support network of understanding individuals who care about your well-being can make a significant difference in your journey toward recovery.

Join a Support Group

In today's interconnected world, one of the remarkable advantages is the ability to connect with others who share similar struggles and experiences. Support groups provide a safe and understanding environment where individuals with OCD can come together to offer mutual support, guidance, and encouragement. By sharing your experiences, listening to others' stories, and learning from their strategies and coping mechanisms, you can gain valuable insights and empowerment to overcome your obsessive compulsions. Being part of a support group fosters a sense of belonging and reminds you that you are not alone in your journey. The collective wisdom and empathy of the group can inspire and motivate you to navigate the challenges of OCD more effectively.

CHAPTER 9: UNDERSTANDING THE UNDERLYING DRIVERS OF ADDICTION AND SUBSTANCE ABUSE

ACT, or Acceptance and Commitment Therapy, holds tremendous relevance in the treatment of addiction because it recognizes the complex nature of addiction and provides a compassionate approach to addressing both the underlying issues and the behaviors associated with it. Addiction is often accompanied by deep-rooted emotional pain, struggles with self-worth, and a sense of disconnection from oneself and others. ACT acknowledges these challenges and offers a path towards healing and transformation.

For individuals trapped in the cycle of addiction, their substance use becomes a means of temporary relief from overwhelming emotions, anxiety, or distressing thoughts. However, the relief is short-lived, and the consequences of addiction can be devastating. ACT encourages individuals to accept the present moment and the discomfort it may bring, rather than relying on substances to escape or avoid these difficult experiences. It invites them to develop a willingness to fully experience their emotions and thoughts without judgment, creating space for self-compassion and growth.

In the context of addiction, individuals may find themselves heavily identified with the role of an addict, which can reinforce a negative self-image and limit their perception of alternative choices. ACT recognizes this over-identification and aims to help individuals broaden their sense of self. Through therapeutic techniques, individuals can detach from the identity of an addict and explore new possibilities for change. By cultivating psychological flexibility, clients can better respond to their thoughts, cravings, and triggers, freeing themselves from the grip of addiction.

Another essential aspect of ACT is the practice of mindfulness. Mindfulness allows individuals to cultivate a non-judgmental awareness of the present moment, including their bodily sensations, emotions, and thoughts related to addiction. By developing a compassionate and curious attitude towards their experience, individuals can observe their urges and cravings without being consumed by them. Mindfulness empowers individuals to make conscious choices and respond skillfully to their internal and external triggers.

ACT also acknowledges the impact of addiction on interpersonal relationships. It recognizes that addiction can lead to isolation, strained connections with loved ones, and a sense of disconnection from social support systems. To address this, ACT emphasizes the importance of fostering meaningful connections and engaging in healthy social interactions. By nurturing relationships with friends and family, individuals can find a sense of belonging, support, and understanding, creating a solid foundation for their recovery journey.

In the therapeutic context, support groups play a vital role in ACT-based treatment for addiction. These groups provide a safe space for individuals to share their experiences, learn from others facing similar challenges, and gain valuable insights and support. Connecting with others who have walked a similar path can be incredibly empowering and can inspire individuals to overcome their addictive patterns. Support groups foster a sense of community, acceptance, and compassion, reminding individuals that they are not alone in their struggles.

ACT recognizes that recovery from addiction is not just about abstaining from substance use but also about aligning one's actions with their core values. It encourages individuals to explore their deeply held values, such as integrity, health, connection, or personal growth, and guides them in making choices that are consistent with these values. By living in alignment with their values, individuals regain a sense of purpose, fulfillment, and authenticity, paving the way for sustainable recovery and a meaningful life beyond addiction.

Through acceptance, mindfulness, psychological flexibility, and the pursuit of value-based actions, ACT offers a comprehensive approach to addiction treatment. It acknowledges the unique challenges faced by individuals battling addiction and provides them with the tools, support, and guidance to reclaim their lives. With empathy and understanding, ACT empowers individuals to break free from the chains of addiction, heal their wounds, and embrace a future filled with hope, connection, and personal growth.

CHAPTER 10: THE TRANSFORMATION THAT OCCURS WHEN YOU QUIT SMOKING

I n 2015, an insightful article by BP Magazine shed light on the profound impact that Acceptance and Commitment Therapy (ACT) can have on individuals struggling with tobacco addiction, particularly among those diagnosed with Bipolar Disorder. The article highlighted a study that delved into the effects of ACT on helping Bipolar Disorder patients quit smoking. This information is especially important considering the prevalence of smoking among individuals with Bipolar Disorder, who are two to three times more likely to smoke compared to the general population but face greater challenges when trying to quit.

The study aimed to assist individuals with mild bipolar symptoms who were also smokers. One group of participants received nicotine patches while engaging in ten ACT sessions conducted over the phone during a 30-day period. Another group attended face-to-face therapy sessions. The results were both intriguing and encouraging. By the end of the month, 30 percent of participants who received in-person therapy reported successfully abstaining from smoking for seven consecutive days. In contrast, only 17 percent of those who underwent phone-based therapy were able to quit smoking. Interestingly, the participants receiving therapy through phone calls did not adhere to the nicotine patch treatment, while 62 percent of the group attending in-person therapy continued to use the patch. Both groups reported a significant 55 percent improvement in their ability to tolerate cigarette cravings.

Another noteworthy study conducted by E. Gifford et al. explored an acceptance-based treatment approach for smoking cessation and compared it to a medical intervention model involving nicotine replacement treatment (NRT) (2004). The study included 76 individuals struggling with nicotine addiction, with 59 percent being female and 41 percent male. The participants came from diverse cultural backgrounds, and over half had completed post-secondary education. It is essential to recognize the unique circumstances of these individuals who found themselves caught in the grip of nicotine addiction. On average, they smoked 21.4 cigarettes per day and had attempted to quit at least four times in the past two years, highlighting the persistent struggle they faced.

The results of the study were exceptionally promising, especially when examined during the one-year follow-up. During the 1960s and 70s, behavior therapy was extensively used to treat smoking addiction, giving rise to various techniques aimed at helping individuals quit smoking (Gifford et al., 2004, 690). However, the efficacy of these methods waned over time, and it became evident that a more comprehensive understanding of the underlying processes and the connection between avoidance and maladaptive coping strategies was necessary.

The study by Gifford et al. was built upon a contextual reasoning and behavior philosophy, acknowledging the intricate nature of smoking addiction. The model employed in the study recognized that smokers often possess the skills to respond in counterproductive ways when faced with challenging internal experiences. Thus, the primary objective of the study was to enhance acceptance skills, alleviate avoidance behaviors, and promote psychological and behavioral flexibility.

These findings demonstrate the power of ACT in addressing tobacco addiction, particularly among individuals with Bipolar Disorder. By fostering acceptance, providing tools to manage cravings, and promoting flexible responses to internal experiences, ACT empowers individuals to navigate the challenges of quitting smoking and embark on a path towards improved health and well-being. It is essential to approach these individuals with empathy, understanding the difficulties they face and offering support as they strive to overcome their addiction and lead fulfilling lives.

With the aim of fostering self-control and empowering individuals on their healing journey, Gifford and their colleagues developed a comprehensive model comprising four key mechanisms:

1. Establishing a Relational Setting: Creating a safe and supportive environment where individuals can explore their experiences openly and without judgment. This relational context allows for a deeper understanding of the factors contributing to their problematic behaviors.

2. Developing Intellectual, Emotional, and Physical Self-Discrimination Skills: Equipping individuals with the ability to identify and differentiate the various aspects of their experiences that have led to negative

behaviors. This skill-building process enables them to pinpoint the triggers and patterns associated with their addictive behaviors.

3. Directly Engaging with Undesirable Experiences: Encouraging individuals to confront and engage with the uncomfortable and unwanted aspects of their experiences. By directly facing these experiences, they learn to reduce avoidance behaviors and find more effective ways to respond.

4. Encouraging Proactive Behavior Initiation: Challenging individuals to initiate positive behaviors that go against their previous maladaptive coping strategies. By taking proactive steps towards healthier choices and actions, individuals gain a sense of control and agency over their lives.

The study compared this approach with Nicotine Replacement Treatment (NRT), which focuses on combating nicotine addiction by alleviating withdrawal symptoms typically experienced when individuals attempt to quit smoking (Gifford et al., 2004, 690). In contrast, the practical procedure model used in ACT aims to address the underlying concerns related to withdrawal and other triggers that lead to avoidance behaviors. By reducing avoidance tendencies, individuals gain increased flexibility to choose alternative pathways towards recovery.

In the NRT group, participants received personalized attention from a trained therapist and a psychotherapy resident who were available around the clock during the treatment period. They were provided with nicotine patches and instructed not to smoke while wearing them. Additionally, they attended an informative session lasting 1.5 hours, including a 30-minute question and answer period. Regular weekly visits to the clinic were scheduled to replace used patches with new ones.

On the other hand, the ACT group engaged in a more intensive treatment approach. They had seven individual sessions with a counselor, each lasting 50 minutes, and participated in seven group sessions lasting 90 minutes over a period of seven weeks. They underwent a comprehensive training program designed to help them recognize their internal triggers and accept the aspects they could not change while simultaneously working towards modifying their behaviors, thoughts, and emotions. They actively practiced helpful activities and exercises tailored to their individual needs.

During the ACT program, we place great emphasis on understanding and supporting individuals on their path to recovery with utmost empathy and compassion. We recognize that addiction is a deeply personal struggle, and it is our mission to provide the tools and support necessary for individuals to navigate their journey of healing.

Let's delve further into the essential aspects of the ACT program that foster this compassionate approach:

1. Exploring Inner and External Factors: We believe in acknowledging the intricate interplay between internal experiences and external circumstances that contribute to addictive behaviors. By understanding the unique challenges individuals face, we can help them gain valuable insights into their struggles and develop effective coping strategies tailored to their specific needs.

2. Challenges with Self-Control: We understand that maintaining control over impulses and addictive behaviors can be incredibly challenging. Our goal is to provide a safe and non-judgmental space for individuals to explore the underlying reasons behind these difficulties. Through this exploration, we can work together to develop healthier and more sustainable self-control strategies.

3. Setting Standards, Goals, and Overcoming Obstacles: We assist individuals in establishing meaningful standards and goals for themselves. Additionally, we understand that obstacles may arise along the way, hindering progress. By identifying and addressing these barriers, we can empower individuals to overcome set-

backs with resilience and perseverance.

4. Embracing Acceptance and Preparedness: We encourage individuals to cultivate acceptance of their current circumstances and embrace the journey of recovery. Acceptance does not imply resignation but rather serves as a foundation for personal growth and transformation. We help individuals develop the readiness and resilience necessary to navigate the challenges they may encounter.

5. Cultivating Mindfulness Skills: Mindfulness is a powerful tool in the recovery process. We introduce individuals to mindfulness techniques that promote present-moment awareness, non-judgmental observation of thoughts and emotions, and conscious responses instead of impulsive reactions. These skills enable individuals to navigate difficult moments with clarity, self-compassion, and a heightened sense of self-awareness.

6. Dealing with Intense Internal Experiences: We provide unwavering support to individuals as they face progressively intense withdrawal symptoms and challenging internal experiences that may arise during their recovery journey. Our therapeutic guidance and nurturing environment empower individuals to develop

resilience and effective strategies for managing these difficulties.

7. Planned Smoking Intervals: We gradually extend the time intervals between smoking-inducing stimuli and the individual's smoking response. This deliberate approach allows individuals to explore new ways of identifying and responding to internal prompts. By reducing reliance on smoking as a coping mechanism, individuals can gradually regain control over their lives.

8. Building Dispersion Skills: Our focus is on developing strategies that disperse addictive thoughts and cravings. We guide individuals in redirecting their focus and attention towards healthier alternatives. Through these skills, individuals gain greater control over their thoughts, reducing the grip of addictive behaviors and paving the way for positive change.

9. Encouraging Behavior Initiation and Accountability: We provide unwavering support to individuals in initiating positive behaviors aligned with their recovery goals. We foster a sense of accountability and empower individuals to take proactive steps towards change. By assuming responsibility for their actions and choices, individuals strengthen their commitment to the recovery process and lay a solid foundation for lasting

change.

By highlighting and embracing these crucial aspects of the ACT program, we create a nurturing and supportive environment where individuals are provided with the necessary tools, insights, and compassionate support they need on their journey of recovery. Our ultimate goal is to empower individuals to embrace change, cultivate self-awareness, and develop effective strategies that lead to a fulfilling life free from the grip of addiction.

CHAPTER 11: FINDING RELIEF FROM CHRONIC PAIN

E xperiencing pain is a fundamental way for the body to communicate with the mind, signaling the need for relief and resolution. However, when pain persists for an extended period, typically over three months, it becomes chronic and significantly impacts the lives of many individuals. In 2010, an estimated seven percent of Americans were affected by enduring pain, prompting extensive research into this complex issue. Chronic pain encompasses a wide range of conditions, from physical ailments to more complex interplay of emotional, biochemical, neurological, and environmental factors. It is in these cases that the mind often misinterprets the pain signals, leading to prolonged and distressing experiences that can feel enigmatic and enduring.

Acceptance and Commitment Therapy practitioners, like Tolman, employ cognitive diffusion techniques to help individuals gain a fresh perspective on their perceived pain. ACT acknowledges the inherent struggle individuals face when confronted with negative thoughts that amplify the pain experience. The instinct to avoid or suppress these thoughts can unintentionally intensify overall suffering. Instead, ACT encourages individuals to embrace the presence of these distressing thoughts while reevaluating their impact, ultimately reducing their disruptive influence. By openly acknowledging and exploring these uncomfortable thoughts, individuals develop emotional resilience and gain the ability to change their behavior and emotions in response to them.

Tolman's concept of acceptance is rooted in the capacity to become an impartial observer of thoughts, acknowledging them without seeking to control or suppress them. This shift in focus allows individuals to relegate thoughts like "Today, the pain is too much to bear" to the background, freeing up mental energy and attention to be directed towards their personal values and goals. By nurturing a mindful detachment from pain-related thoughts, individuals can regain agency over their lives and prioritize what truly matters to them.

Extensive research has shed light on the remarkable potential of Acceptance and Commitment Therapy in alleviating chronic pain. Unlike traditional approaches that solely focus on directly targeting or eliminating physical pain symptoms, ACT takes a holistic approach by addressing the psychological and emotional aspects associated with pain. This empathetic approach recognizes that chronic pain is not just a physical sensation but a multifaceted experience that affects all aspects of a person's life.

For many individuals living with chronic pain, the instinctual response is to resist and fight against the pain, hoping to conquer it. However, this resistance often backfires, intensifying the pain and exacerbating the suffering. ACT offers a different perspective by helping individuals reduce the influence of negative pain-related thoughts. By acknowledging and accepting the presence of pain, individuals can adopt a more adaptive mindset that allows them to function more effectively in their daily lives.

One powerful aspect of ACT is its emphasis on redirecting attention towards meaningful goals and values. By identifying what truly matters to them, individuals can prioritize those aspects of life that bring joy and fulfillment, even in the face of chronic pain. For example, a person limited by chronic pain may find solace and motivation in spending quality time with their grandchildren. By consciously shifting their focus towards this cherished goal, they not only experience the joy of those moments but also recognize the inherent value in them. This shift in perspective and reevaluation of what is truly important can significantly diminish the impact of persistent pain on their overall well-being.

Through ACT, individuals learn to navigate their pain experience with compassion, understanding, and self-acceptance. It empowers them to develop coping strategies that acknowledge the reality of chronic pain while embracing a broader range of possibilities for leading a fulfilling life. By fostering resilience and empowering individuals to reclaim their lives from the grips of pain, ACT offers hope and support to those living with chronic pain.

Studies consistently reveal a significant correlation between acceptance and the experience of chronic pain. Lower levels of acceptance tend to be associated with greater pain intensity, while higher levels of acceptance are linked to decreased pain perception. Patient diaries and research on cognitive behavioral therapy (CBT) further support these findings, indicating that engaging in thought activities that are beneficial can improve mood and boost patients' confidence in managing their pain.

ACT interventions that promote acceptance and values-based approaches have demonstrated promising results in altering pain management strategies and aiding individuals in coping with chronic pain. Additionally, investigations into the relationship between insomnia and chronic pain suggest that individuals with higher levels of psychological flexibility experience less sleep disturbance. However, it is worth noting that acceptance may present challenges for individuals with mental disorders related to chronic pain, as they may fear exacerbating their condition. Customizing ACT interventions to address these specific concerns becomes crucial in such cases.

The effectiveness of ACT extends across diverse populations. Studies have shown positive outcomes among Iranian women suffering from chronic headaches and groups consisting of both young and elderly individuals with chronic pain. L. M. McCracken, a practitioner utilizing ACT in the treatment of chronic pain, places emphasis on the importance of mindfulness and acceptance of distressing thoughts, sensations, and emotions in the present moment. This approach empowers individuals to directly confront their pain experience while cultivating an accepting and compassionate attitude towards themselves.

In a comprehensive three-year follow-up study conducted by McCracken and Vowles in Bath, England, over 75 percent of the participants reported positive outcomes through acceptance-based interventions. The study involved 28 individuals, with each student therapist treating two patients using either CBT or ACT. The findings indicated that acceptance emerged as the most critical factor leading to positive results in both groups. This study underscores the value of acceptance and its practical application in improving the well-being of individuals living with chronic pain.

Mental treatment methods for chronic pain, such as psychological flexibility and acceptance, emphasize the importance of confronting discomfort and consciously adapting to challenging situations. Psychotherapists trained in these approaches strive to be empathetic and supportive of individuals enduring pain, providing guidance and understanding as they navigate their unique journeys with compassion. By incorporating acceptance-based techniques and fostering psychological resilience, individuals can find new ways to manage their pain, regain control, and enhance their overall quality of life.

CHAPTER 12: SIMPLE MINDFULNESS EXERCISES FOR EVERYDAY LIFE

Exploring the Power of Mindfulness in Therapy Sessions

Mindfulness serves as a vital component of Acceptance and Commitment Therapy, bringing a heightened level of awareness and presence to the therapeutic process. It is crucial to introduce mindfulness techniques early on in the therapy program, allowing both the client and therapist to determine the most effective methods for each individual's circumstances, as suggested by Hayes and Lillis (2012, 97). Simply asking the client to close their eyes is not sufficient; additional exercises can be assigned for them to practice at home.

Incorporating mindfulness exercises at the beginning of each therapy session can be immensely beneficial (Hayes and Lillis, 98). Guiding the client to bring their attention to the present moment, instructing them to close their eyes, and grounding their feet on the floor can establish a foundation of attentiveness for the entire 50-minute session.

Engaging in mindfulness walks can also be valuable, as proposed by Hayes and Lillis (ibid.). The therapist may choose to accompany the client on these walks or encourage the client to undertake them independently. During these walks, the individual is encouraged to focus their attention on a specific aspect of their environment for a brief period, perhaps one or two minutes at a time.

While practicing mindfulness exercises, it can be beneficial for the therapist to suggest that the client visualizes placing their thoughts, feelings, and sensations into metaphorical boxes (ibi d.). This practice allows the client to create a sense of separation between themselves and their internal experiences, fostering a greater sense of detachment and acceptance.

According to Luoma, Hayes, and Walser (2017, 137), without a more advanced form of mindfulness, patients may struggle to connect with their sense of self without self-evaluation. The internal language they use, such as labeling themselves as "lonely" or "short," can blur the distinction between the self as the observer and the self as the observed. By cultivating a connection with the present moment, individuals can begin to view themselves as a constantly evolving and fluid self-in-process.

Structured mindfulness exercises offer individuals a deeper understanding of their self-as-process. One such exercise is the Floating Leaves on a Moving Stream (ibid.). Clients imagine themselves at the edge of a stream, observing leaves gently floating by. Each thought is envisioned as being placed on a floating leaf. If a thought starts to carry them away, they consciously bring themselves back to the task of placing thoughts on leaves. The therapist can inquire if the client's mind tends to wander along the stream. Similarly, this exercise can be adapted using different imagery, such as cars passing on a road.

Another alternative exercise involves visualizing clouds drifting across the sky (Luoma, Hayes, and Walser, 2012, 138). The client imagines themselves lying on a green field, gazing up at the sky. They assign each thought to a passing cloud, using either words or images. If their mind begins to wander, the client gently redirects their focus back to the clouds.

After each mindfulness exercise, engaging in a discussion about the client's experience can be highly beneficial. This allows for reflection, exploration of any insights gained, and the opportunity to integrate these experiences into their overall therapeutic journey.

Discovering the Healing Power of Meditation

Meditation can offer valuable support on the path to healing. Clients can engage in mindfulness meditation exercises from the comfort of their own homes, utilizing a variety of resources such as CDs, books, and online platforms that offer different meditation styles. According to Hershfield (The OCD Stories, 2016), meditation involves directing one's attention to a chosen focal point and noticing when the mind begins to wander, then gently redirecting it back to the present moment.

When incorporating mindfulness and meditation exercises into therapy, it is crucial to carefully tailor them to each patient's specific needs and experiences. For instance, individuals with a challenging childhood may benefit more from eyes-open meditation exercises, as closing their eyes might evoke distressing images from their past.

As therapy progresses and mental flexibility improves, the practice of meditation becomes even more powerful. Hershfield suggests that just ten minutes of meditation each day can have a significant positive impact (ibid.). Making meditation a regular part of one's daily routine is ideal, especially when complemented by other mindfulness techniques. By pausing and truly experiencing the present moment, whether it's observing the road ahead or savoring a song or the taste of food, mindfulness can be practiced anywhere and anytime. This allows individuals to cultivate mastery over their attention and life, as noted by Hershfield (ibid.). Mindfulness empowers individuals to have greater control over their actions and responses, particularly when it comes to managing anger.

It is worth mentioning that many Western individuals who practice meditation may associate it with a particular faith or spiritual belief system. Hayes (The OCD Stories) acknowledges that some individuals may view meditation solely through that lens and believe it should only be practiced within a spiritual or religious framework. However, Hayes emphasizes that embracing an entire belief system is not a prerequisite for reaping the benefits of meditation for overall well-being.

In the context of healing, meditation is a nonspiritual life skill. It is not the specific method or technique of meditation that holds utmost importance, according to Hayes. Instead, meditation is utilized to foster greater authenticity, flexibility, and personal values (The OCD Stories, n.d.). It can serve as a transformative tool, helping patients become the person they aspire to be, aligning their actions and choices with their true selves.

Embracing Mindfulness: Cultivating Calmness in Daily Life

In the midst of our busy and chaotic lives, finding moments of rest and connection with our inner selves may seem like an impossible task. However, it is crucial for our well-being, both physically and mentally. Pocket Mindfulness, a website dedicated to mindfulness practices, understands the importance of staying mindful and offers six practical guidelines to incorporate into your day-to-day routine.

- Breathing: Take a moment to pause and focus on your breath. Inhale deeply through your nose, allowing the breath to fill your lungs and expand your abdomen. As you exhale through your mouth, release any tension or stress you may be holding in your body. Pay attention to the sensation of the breath as it flows in and out, noticing the gentle rise and fall of your chest. With each breath, let go of all thoughts and worries, allowing yourself to be fully present in the experience of breathing. As you continue to breathe consciously, let your attention travel through your body, bringing awareness to any areas of tension or discomfort and allowing them to soften and release. Notice the energy around you, the subtle movements in the air, and the sensations within your body as you breathe. This practice of conscious breathing can help anchor you in the present moment, promoting a sense of calm and centeredness.

- Observation: Connect with the beauty and wonder of the natural world by choosing an ordinary object in your immediate surroundings and dedicating a few minutes to observing it mindfully. It could be a simple flower, a tree, or even a mundane household item. Take the time to really see it as if you are seeing it for the first time. Notice its shape, color, texture, and any intricate details. Pay attention to how it makes you feel and the sensations it evokes within you. As you observe, allow yourself to be fully present in the moment, letting go of any distractions or thoughts about the past or future. Engage all your senses in the experience, noticing the subtle sounds, smells, and even the taste of the air around you. By immersing yourself in the observation of this object, you cultivate a sense of awe and appreciation for the beauty and intricacy of the world we often take for granted.

- Awareness: Choose a simple and seemingly insignificant daily task, such as opening a door, and approach it with mindful awareness. As you perform the action, bring your full attention to every movement and sensation involved. Notice the touch of the doorknob or handle in your hand, feeling its texture and temperature. Observe the movement of your arm and the subtle shifts in your body as you open the door. Allow yourself to become fully engaged in the experience, savoring each moment without rushing. Notice any thoughts or emotions that arise during this simple act, and practice non-judgmental awareness by acknowledging them and letting them pass without clinging to them. This awareness can extend to other repetitive activities throughout your day, such as eating, walking, or even brushing your teeth. By infusing these routine actions with mindful attention, you bring a sense of purpose and appreciation to your daily life, enhancing your connection to the present moment.

- Listening: This exercise invites you to cultivate deep presence and let go of the influence of past experiences and assumptions. Select a piece of music that you have never listened to before. Find a quiet and comfortable space, put on your headphones, and close your eyes. Allow yourself to fully immerse in the music, approaching it with a beginner's mind. Let go of any preconceived notions or judgments about the genre, artist, or title. Instead, focus on the sound itself, listening with a sense of curiosity and openness. Notice

126

the various instruments, melodies, rhythms, and harmonies that weave together to create the music. If there are lyrics, pay attention to the nuances of the vocalist's voice and the emotions conveyed. Allow the music to wash over you, engaging your senses and inviting you to be fully present in the sonic experience. By practicing deep listening, you can let go of the noise of the mind and find refuge in the present moment.

- Immersion: In this exercise, you are encouraged to find serenity and fulfillment by fully engaging in a simple activity. Choose a task that you often consider mundane or routine, such as washing dishes, folding laundry, or sweeping the floor. Rather than approaching it as a chore to be completed quickly, bring your complete attention to every detail of the activity. Notice the feel of the water on your hands, the texture of the fabric as you fold it, or the rhythmic movements of the broom as you sweep. Be fully present in each moment, allowing yourself to appreciate the small intricacies and subtleties of the task at hand. See it as a brand-new experience, even if you've done it countless times before. By immersing yourself in the activity, mentally, bodily, and psychologically, you create a space for mindfulness and contentment to emerge. Each action becomes an opportunity for presence and self-discovery, reminding you to find joy in the simplicity of daily life.

- Cultivating Appreciation: Take a moment to pause and shift your focus towards the things in your day that often go unnoticed or underappreciated. It's time to express gratitude for the ordinary, seemingly insignificant elements that make up our lives. These can be objects or individuals that are an integral part of your daily existence. Begin by observing your surroundings and consciously selecting five things that you tend to overlook or take for granted. It could be the people around you, such as family members, friends, or coworkers, who contribute to your well-being and support you in various ways. Express genuine appreciation for their presence and the positive impact they have on your life. In addition to individuals, consider the inanimate objects that often blend into the background of your daily routine. Reflect on the simple yet essential items that facilitate your comfort and convenience, like water taps, electrical cables, or household appliances. Acknowledge their role in providing you with the basic necessities and comforts of life. Expand your appreciation further to include elements of nature that surround you, such as plants, trees, or flowers. These living beings add beauty and a sense of vitality to your environment. Take a moment to notice their presence, their colors, and the intricate details that make them unique. Even the mundane aspects of urban life, like pavements and vans, deserve recognition. They serve as functional components of our urban landscape, facilitating our mobility and daily activities. Acknowledge the role they play in supporting your daily routines and enabling you to navigate through the world. By intentionally directing your attention towards these often overlooked aspects of life, you bring a renewed sense of gratitude and awareness. Recognize the interconnectedness of all these elements and how they contribute to your overall well-being and the fabric of your existence.

In the therapeutic relationship, descriptions play a crucial role in helping you gain a deeper understanding of your own inner workings. They serve as powerful tools to illuminate the intricate landscape of your thoughts, emotions, and experiences. By exploring these descriptions, you can embark on a journey of self-discovery and self-awareness. Let's explore a few of them together:

The Sailing Boat Metaphor: Navigating Life's Challenges

Imagine yourself as the captain of a sailing boat, navigating the vast ocean. As you sail, waves occasionally splash onto the deck, soaking your feet. To address this, you have a bucket onboard that you can use to bail out the unwanted water.

On a calm and sunny day, unexpectedly, a massive wave crashes onto the boat, causing water to flood in. Now, it becomes crucial for you to start bailing once again. It's a routine task that comes with sailing, and you approach it with serenity and mindfulness. However, as time passes, you begin to feel tense and insecure. Your movements become frantic, your heart races, and anxiety creeps in, fueled by the fear of what might happen if you don't empty the water quickly enough.

In the midst of your suffering, you become disconnected from the overall navigation and direction of your boat. You lose sight of where it's going and how it's being steered. Perhaps you've been so consumed by bailing that you've neglected the essential task of navigating. You've lost control of the vessel.

Now, shift your attention to the bucket. You realize that it's not an ordinary bucket but a filter full of holes. This realization raises a question: What can you do in this situation?

Ordinarily, once you finish bailing, you would be in a position to correct the course of your boat. However, with an inadequate tool, you find yourself trapped in a cycle of stress, futilely expending energy, and intensifying your actions. It's like a hamster on a wheel, exerting effort without making real progress. All this energy could be more effectively utilized if you had a functional bucket.

The crucial question to ask yourself in this metaphorical scenario is: Which scenario would you prefer? Would you rather be in a boat with minimal water, but sailing in the wrong direction? Or would you prefer to be water-logged but traveling in the direction you desire? With the right tools, you can both navigate towards your desired destination and effectively manage the water that comes your way.

This metaphorical comparison can help you envision the effectiveness of various life strategies or coping mechanisms. Just like the bucket and the filter, certain problem-solving tools may be more beneficial than others. Sometimes, people eagerly avoid discomfort or temporary inconveniences, like having wet feet, only to create greater problems in the long run. By adopting a different perspective, you may come to realize that having wet feet, metaphorically speaking, is not as significant as it may initially seem.

By exploring this metaphor, therapists can help clients gain insights into their life experiences and discover more effective ways of navigating challenges. It encourages a shift in perspective and invites clients to reassess their priorities and choices, ultimately empowering them to make more informed decisions that align with their desired direction in life.

Confronting the Mind Bully: Overcoming Inner Struggles

Let's delve into the concept of the Mind Bully, which holds particular significance for individuals grappling with annoyance, nervousness, or despair. The Mind Bully symbolizes a formidable problem that many of us face. Picture yourself holding a rope over a deep pit, with the Mind Bully gripping the other end, determined to drag you into the chasm.

However, here's an important realization: The Mind Bully can only inflict harm if you give credence to its words. As you hold onto the rope, you find yourself listening intently to the monster's vocalizations, paying attention to its every sound. Paying attention to the Mind Bully implies placing trust in its influence. It thrives on the energy you devote to it, nourishing its power.

Now, let's take a moment to reflect on what would happen if you were to release your grip and let the rope drop. What would become of the Mind Bully?

It would still be there before you, continuing to unleash horrifying and mean-spirited remarks. However, unlike when you held onto the rope, it would no longer have the ability to pull you closer to the pit. If we stop feeding the monster, it gradually loses its magnificence and loudness.

We have the power to disempower issues such as nervousness or despair by redirecting our attention. While it is essential to acknowledge and recognize their presence, we can detach ourselves from their grip and place less trust in their influence. Engaging in mindfulness exercises can facilitate a swift shift in our mindset, allowing us to let go of despairing thoughts or anxious concerns. By doing so, we stay on track to achieve what we truly desire.

Remember, you hold the ability to overcome the Mind Bully within you. By shifting your attention and employing mindfulness techniques, you can reclaim control over your thoughts and emotions, paving the way for personal growth and achievement.

Navigating the Quicksand: Embracing Challenges and Finding Strength

Let's explore the metaphor of quicksand, which sheds light on our struggles and how we can overcome them. Quicksand is a treacherous blend of wet sand that cannot bear much weight. Stepping into it, you find yourself sinking, unable to find a stable footing on the shifting ground.

Here's an important truth: The more you fight against quicksand, the further it pulls you down. Each struggle intensifies the descent, and attempting to climb out only leads to futility.

Your attempts to use stepladders or force your way out become counterproductive, as they only sink you deeper into the sandy trap.

So, how do individuals extricate themselves from quicksand? They spread their body weight over a larger surface area. They lie down, accepting the predicament they find themselves in instead of resisting it. It may seem counterintuitive, but it holds a profound truth: Engaging in a fight against quicksand only allows the quicksand to emerge as the victor.

The lesson here is that accepting your condition and ceasing to resist its presence sets the stage for your escape. In a similar vein, pain and grief can deceive us much like quicksand. It's natural to resist unpleasant internal experiences, but the more we struggle against them, the deeper we sink in the quagmire of life.

Embracing your pain and grief is the first step towards transcending them. It enables you to construct a solid plan of action based on a thorough understanding of your emotions. Acknowledging that agony is an inherent part of life can be challenging, but it allows you to emerge from the experience stronger and more resilient.

Remember, dear friend, you have the capacity to face sorrow head-on and emerge from it with newfound strength. By embracing the challenges that life presents, you open yourself up to growth, resilience, and the opportunity to build a brighter future.

CHAPTER 13: HOLISTIC APPROACHES TO TRACKING YOUR WEIGHT LOSS JOURNEY

T raditional weight loss treatments often fall short in providing sustainable and long-term results, as highlighted by Lillis and Kendra (2014). They suggest that Acceptance and Commitment Therapy may hold more promise for achieving lasting weight loss outcomes. ACT can be used as a complementary or integrated approach alongside other treatment modalities. However, further research is needed to validate this proposition.

Many weight loss programs focus on rigid schedules of fasting, exercise, and social therapy, resulting in an average weight loss of eight to ten percent over six months (Lillis and Kendra, 2014, 1). Unfortunately, individuals who undergo these programs often experience weight regain, with one-third of participants gaining back the lost weight within the first year and more than 100 percent within five years (ibid.). Additionally, up to 30 percent of individuals do not complete these programs, indicating the need for more effective and sustainable treatments.

Factors such as binge eating, mental distress, feelings of inadequacy, negative body image, and low quality of life contribute to the erosion of weight loss program effectiveness (ibid.). Lillis and Kendra identify psychosocial stressors, disinhibition, emotional eating in response to stress, depression, and feelings of food-related deprivation as predictors of weight gain.

In this context, mindfulness and meditation techniques hold potential for advancing weight loss treatments. These approaches focus on changing an individual's relationship with intrusive or distressing internal experiences.

Lillis and Kendra challenge the conventional approach to addressing obesity, known as standard behavioral treatment (SBT), which is rooted in learning theory (ibid.). SBT emphasizes modifying the environmental factors that trigger maladaptive behaviors. It involves self-monitoring of behaviors, setting personal goals, and tracking factors such as food intake and exercise availability. Cognitive interventions aim to identify and challenge maladaptive thoughts, while promoting weight loss strategies and goals. Techniques like thought-stopping and anxiety reduction are commonly used.

Drawing a comparison between SBT and ACT, Lillis and Kendra emphasize that both approaches involve skill-building. Therapeutic education can be conducted at home or in group settings, focusing on practical skills like regular self-weighing aligned with the individual's actual weight. These skills empower individuals to develop new behavioral patterns and monitoring practices to support their weight loss journey.

While ACT originates from the social change movement, its perspective on learned behaviors related to obesity differs from approaches like SBT. Grounded in Relational Frame Theory (RFT), ACT recognizes the role of language in shaping detrimental behavioral patterns and focuses on how language can amplify mental distress. Merely recalling an instance of ridicule, for example, can trigger significant pain on its own, highlighting the power of language in creating emotional turmoil.

ACT also acknowledges that individuals often try to avoid pain, and their thoughts and emotions surrounding pain can become experiences they seek to evade. For instance, the mere thought of swimming may induce anxiety, fear of judgment, feelings of inadequacy, and self-criticism, leading individuals to avoid swimming altogether. This pattern of avoidance is pervasive in various psychological and behavioral health issues, including weight problems. Attempting to escape undesirable internal experiences often leads to emotional eating as a way to alleviate negative moods, which, in turn, exacerbates weight gain and perpetuates the cycle of distress. Furthermore, the shame associated with overeating can fuel maladaptive coping strategies.

ACT employs six processes to help individuals acknowledge and accept their dislikes, negative emotions, actions, and thoughts. It emphasizes the importance of setting standards and values-based goals that foster positive behavior change. The ultimate goal of ACT is to enhance overall well-being and lead a more fulfilling life, rather than solely focusing on weight loss or prevention of weight gain. Healthy living is defined by personal standards such as engaging in family life, achieving educational milestones, securing meaningful employment, and more. By shifting the client's focus away from food and weight, ACT encourages them to concentrate on aligning their behaviors with their values and goals. It prompts clients to explore the consequences of not engaging in exercise or neglecting their diet, raising awareness about the conflict between their aspirations and their actions. Thus, ACT fosters a shift in perspective, emphasizing behavioral change rather than criticizing eating habits or lack of exercise.

Research indicates that ACT can be successful in improving self-esteem and serving as a treatment approach for weight loss and maintenance. Lillis and Kendra (2014) propose that a combination of therapies, incorporating elements of honesty, mindfulness exercises, and values work, along with specific actions like dieting and exercise, can yield positive outcomes. They suggest that reframing the daily caloric quota, which may initially seem daunting for many individuals struggling with weight, can be viewed in a more optimistic light. Moreover, the potential rewards associated with aligning behavior with personal standards, such as increased self-respect, improved self-image, and positive social interactions, can serve as powerful motivators. Studies supporting the integration of different approaches have emerged in recent years, as mentioned by Lillis and Kendra.

While Lillis and Kendra propose a model that combines SBT and ACT, one challenge lies in reconciling the divergent overarching goals of each approach. Additionally, shared weight loss activities, such as daily weigh-ins, can reinforce negative individual experiences. Therefore, weight loss methods, including dietary and exercise regimens, must be integrated within a comprehensive program. Addressing food cravings within the context of ACT poses another challenge, as anxiety associated with monitoring past cravings may trigger problematic thoughts, emotions, and behaviors. Even a simple task like grocery shopping may require adjustments to align with the principles of ACT. Effective implementation of a combined program would necessitate adapting teaching methods and discussions to align with ACT principles.

In conclusion, Lillis and Kendra recommend exploring multiple programs and monitoring their outcomes to determine the most effective treatment approach for weight loss. Taking a compassionate and multifaceted approach, incorporating ACT principles along with practical strategies, can pave the way for meaningful and sustainable weight loss journeys.

CHAPTER 14: EMPOWERING SELF-CARE FOR DIABETES MANAGEMENT

I n a compassionate and insightful study by Laura Melton (2016, 211-213), she delves into the application of ACT for individuals with diabetes. Recognizing that diabetes patients face not only the physical challenges but also emotional burdens, Melton emphasizes the need for a comprehensive approach that goes beyond traditional medical treatment.

In her paper, Melton highlights the following key aspects:

Building Competence and Enhancing Diabetes Management: The program focuses on equipping individuals with the necessary skills and knowledge to effectively manage their diabetes. This includes strategies for monitoring blood sugar levels, making informed dietary choices, and engaging in regular physical activity.

Embracing Group Support: Recognizing the power of a supportive community, the program adopts a group-based approach. This allows participants to share their experiences, provide mutual encouragement, and learn from one another's successes and challenges.

Reducing Stigma and Promoting Inclusion: Melton emphasizes the importance of creating a stigma-free environment where individuals with diabetes can feel accepted and supported. This inclusive approach fosters a sense of belonging and encourages active participation in managing their condition.

Time Commitment and Dedication: Participating in the program requires a commitment of time and effort. By dedicating themselves to the program, individuals can fully immerse in the learning process and reap the benefits of improved diabetes self-management.

By addressing these essential components, the ACT program aims to empower individuals with diabetes to take control of their health and well-being, enabling them to lead fulfilling lives while effectively managing their condition.

In a compassionate effort to address the unique challenges faced by individuals with diabetes, the combination of six ACT procedures proved to be highly beneficial. Recognizing that not all participants were familiar with ACT at the beginning of the program, a comprehensive overview of each procedure was provided in the initial meeting. Over the course of four workshops, the focus was placed on different aspects of the ACT model.

The first meeting centered around exploring personal values and the importance of living in the present moment. The second workshop delved into the power of cognitive defusion and acceptance, incorporating mindfulness exercises to enhance self-awareness. The third workshop introduced the concept of self-as-context and the art of self-observation. Each session built upon the previous ones, reinforcing the core principles of ACT and their application to diabetes management. Participants concluded the workshops by identifying their personal values and engaging in a dedicated action exercise.

While this investigational program demonstrated the potential benefits of ACT, it is important to note that only a small number of participants attended all the meetings. However, Jennifer Gregg, Steven Hayes, and Glenn Callaghan have developed a guide for treating diabetes with ACT, which can be accessed on the San Jose State University website. Their intention is to provide more than just education to diabetes patients, recognizing the need for holistic approaches to living with the condition. They outline two key resolutions:

1. Treatment Approach: By addressing emotions, providing education, and fostering cognitive flexibility, individuals can differentiate between aspects of their diabetes management that are within their control and those that are not.

2. Versatile Delivery: The method and treatment should be adaptable to meet the diverse needs of healthcare professionals and their patients.

Living with diabetes can bring forth a range of undesirable emotions, thoughts, and behaviors. Receiving a diabetes diagnosis can be devastating for some individuals, and the necessary lifestyle changes can cause anxiety and worry. Gregg, Hayes, and Callaghan highlight the specific lifestyle adjustments that diabetes patients must navigate, including carefully monitoring their food choices, regularly checking blood glucose levels, and engaging in regular exercise to improve insulin utilization.

Managing diabetes becomes particularly challenging for individuals with obesity, sedentary habits, and a preference for sugary foods. In addition to adhering to medical instructions and making significant dietary changes, anticipating the difficulties and daily realities of living with diabetes presents an additional hurdle. Naturally, avoidance becomes a potential concern. Recognizing that food can serve as a coping mechanism for painful emotions and thoughts, and that high-carbohydrate foods are often seen as a source of relief, addressing avoidance is vital for individuals with diabetes to effectively navigate their condition and improve their overall well-being.

Having diabetes can undoubtedly bring about feelings of uneasiness and worries. In line with the empathetic perspective of ACT, a comprehensive therapeutic treatment program was designed to empower individuals with diabetes to improve their self-management. The program consists of two main components: education on living with diabetes and targeted interventions to enhance motivation and self-acceptance. To facilitate this process, the program is divided into five modules:

Module I: Education and Information
Module II: Food, Diabetes, and Your Health
Module III: Exercise and Diabetes
Module IV: Coping and Stress Management
Module V: Acceptance and Action

These modules are conducted in a group therapy setting, with skilled clinicians serving as group leaders. The provided guide offers a range of practical strategies and skill-building activities. Participants are encouraged to use registration and self-assessment forms to track their progress, access informative fact sheets, and explore various topics such as mindfulness. Additionally, the guide includes instructions on managing overall well-being, including foot care, as well as values questionnaires to help individuals align their actions with their personal values. To further support self-reflection, there are questionnaires available to record thoughts and emotions, along with unit plans to guide participants throughout the program. Finally, the guide includes a questionnaire for setting and documenting personal goals.

This comprehensive resource aims to provide individuals with the tools and knowledge needed to effectively manage their diabetes while fostering a sense of understanding and empowerment. Through group therapy and a variety of engaging resources, the program encourages individuals to take an active role in their self-care journey and promotes a compassionate and supportive environment.

CHAPTER 15: EMPOWERING STRATEGIES FOR MANAGING STRESS

M ental stress is a complex experience that encompasses various forms of emotional pain. However, it's important to recognize that not all stress is inherently negative. In fact, mild levels of stress can serve as a motivating force, encouraging individuals to accomplish tasks, solve problems, and stay focused. It plays a role in adaptation and helps individuals respond to the demands of their social and physical environments. This type of stress is known as positive stress.

On the other hand, excessive or prolonged stress can have detrimental effects on mental and physical well-being. It has been linked to the development of mental disorders, as well as serious physical conditions such as strokes, ulcers, and heart attacks. Stress can stem from external factors, but it can also be triggered by internal thoughts, negative emotions, and behaviors. When individuals feel overwhelmed and lack confidence in their ability to cope, stress can feel overwhelming and intimidating.

Certain situations are particularly prone to causing severe stress. Examples include natural disasters, wars, failing important exams, experiencing or witnessing a severe injury or accident, or going through a breakup. Significant life changes like graduating, relocating, getting married, or starting a new job can also generate high levels of stress.

The duration of stress is another crucial factor. When stressors persist for weeks, months, or even years, the accumulated stress can take a toll on both the body and mind. Additionally, decision-making processes can contribute to feelings of stress for many individuals.

It's essential to remember that stress is subjective and varies from person to person. For example, public speaking may be enjoyable for one person (Person A), while another person (Person B) may find it highly stressful. Each individual has their own unique way of handling daily annoyances, and what may be manageable for one person could be a significant source of stress for another. Furthermore, individuals employ various internal strategies to avoid or reduce stress based on their own perceptions and coping mechanisms. It is crucial to acknowledge these differences and respect each person's experiences and responses to stress.

Managing conflicts that produce stress can be a daunting task, and it's completely understandable to feel overwhelmed in such situations. Let's explore the three approaches to stress-producing conflicts in more detail:

- *Approach-approach conflict:* Imagine finding yourself torn between two equally appealing options. It can be challenging to make a decision when both choices hold significant value or bring you joy. For instance, you might feel torn between attending a much-anticipated concert or staying in to watch a highly anticipated movie. It's natural to experience a sense of excitement and hesitation when faced with such a delightful dilemma.

- *Avoidance-avoidance conflict:* Sometimes, life presents us with situations where we must choose between two unappealing options. These decisions can be particularly difficult as both choices seem equally unwanted. For instance, you might face the tough decision of accepting another loan with unfavorable terms to pay off a mortgage or facing the possibility of foreclosure on your beloved home. It's completely understandable to feel stressed and anxious when confronted with such unfavorable choices.

- *Approach-avoidance conflict:* This type of conflict arises when you must make a decision about an option that has both positive and negative aspects. It can be quite challenging to weigh the pros and cons and arrive at a resolution. For example, you might contemplate attending an expensive school that offers exceptional education and promising post-graduation employment prospects. However, this decision would require you to borrow funds, adding financial pressure to your life. It's natural to experience a mix of excitement and apprehension when grappling with such conflicting factors.

Apart from conflicts, stress often accompanies travel experiences, and it's essential to acknowledge the potential difficulties that can arise. Travelers may find themselves stressed due to various factors such as lost luggage, unexpected delays that disrupt plans, or simply feeling out of their comfort zones. Being in unfamiliar surroundings can naturally evoke feelings of unease and anxiety. It's important to approach these stressors with self-compassion and patience, recognizing that navigating unfamiliar territories can be challenging for anyone.

Moreover, there are stressors that exist within our environment, which can impact our well-being without us even realizing it. Pollution, crowded spaces, harsh lighting, and excessive noise are just a few examples of environmental stressors that can contribute to our overall stress levels. It's crucial to be mindful of these external factors and make efforts to create environments that promote calmness and well-being.

To alleviate the negative effects of stress, incorporating mindfulness and acceptance techniques into our lives can be beneficial. Cultivating mindfulness involves staying present in the moment, acknowledging our emotions and thoughts without judgment. Acceptance involves recognizing that stress is a natural part of life and learning to embrace it rather than fighting against it. These practices can empower us to navigate stressful situations with greater resilience and compassion towards ourselves.

In more significant manifestations of stress, the principles of Acceptance and Commitment Therapy (ACT) can be applied to provide effective strategies for managing and reducing stress. ACT emphasizes six essential processes that guide individuals in uncovering stressors, gaining self-awareness, and cultivating psychological flexibility. By developing a deeper understanding of the thoughts and emotions that contribute to stress, individuals can begin to develop a more compassionate and accepting relationship with themselves.

Through identifying personal standards, individuals can clarify their values and aspirations, enabling them to approach conflicts and irritating factors with a more constructive perspective. Prioritizing goals aligned with one's values empowers individuals to shift their focus from stress-inducing thoughts to actions that promote personal growth and well-being.

When it comes to reducing stress, there are several methods that you may already be familiar with. Let's explore these strategies further:

- Engage in regular exercise: Implementing a consistent exercise routine can significantly contribute to stress reduction. Aim for at least four or five exercise sessions per week, incorporating activities that you enjoy and that align with your physical abilities. Exercise not only helps release tension from your body but also stimulates the production of endorphins, which are natural mood boosters. Whether it's going for a walk, practicing yoga, or engaging in any form of physical activity that resonates with you, make it a priority to carve out time for exercise.

- Build a support network: Surrounding yourself with a supportive network of family, friends, or peers can be invaluable in managing stress. Sharing your feelings and experiences with trusted individuals can provide comfort, guidance, and a sense of belonging. Lean on your support network during challenging times, allowing them to offer assistance, lend a listening ear, or simply provide a source of comfort and encouragement. Remember, you don't have to face stress alone.

- Establish a structured routine: Creating a structured schedule can help bring a sense of order and predictability to your daily life. Consider organizing your time by developing a timetable or to-do lists that outline your tasks and responsibilities. Breaking down your day into manageable chunks can alleviate feelings of overwhelm and provide a sense of control. Allow for a healthy balance between work or study commitments, leisure activities, self-care, and rest.

- Practice relaxation and visualization techniques: Incorporating relaxation and visualization exercises into your routine can help calm your mind and body. These techniques involve consciously focusing on relaxing your muscles, deep breathing, and visualizing peaceful and positive images. Engaging in activities such as meditation, mindfulness, or guided imagery can provide a much-needed respite from stress and allow you to cultivate a sense of inner calm.

- Release muscle tension: Pay attention to your body and make a conscious effort to release tension in your muscles. You can try progressive muscle relaxation exercises, where you systematically tense and then relax different muscle groups in your body. Another option is engaging in activities like stretching, yoga, or massage therapy, which can promote physical and mental relaxation.

- Build confidence through effective communication: Enhancing your communication skills and assertiveness can contribute to reducing stress in various situations. Learning how to express your thoughts, feelings, and needs assertively, while also actively listening to others, can lead to healthier and more fulfilling interactions. Effective communication fosters understanding, promotes problem-solving, and minimizes conflicts, thereby reducing potential stressors in your relationships.

- Expressive writing and reflection: Maintaining a diary or journal can serve as an outlet for expressing and reflecting on your true emotions and thoughts.

Writing down your experiences, concerns, and joys can help you gain clarity and perspective. Additionally, it provides a safe space for self-expression, allowing you to process and release pent-up emotions. Regularly engaging in this practice can contribute to emotional well-being and serve as a valuable tool for self-reflection.

- Explore workplace stress management programs: Many workplaces offer programs or resources specifically designed to address stress management. Take advantage of these opportunities and inquire about available workshops, counseling services, or wellness initiatives. These programs often provide practical strategies and support for coping with work-related stressors, fostering a healthier work environment.

In the realm of stress management, there are various approaches that can be applied, particularly when it comes to addressing workplace stress (Lockhart, 2018). It's important to navigate change by acknowledging its potential benefits, which can help alleviate some of the fear associated with it. Additionally, seeking assistance and resources can be beneficial when feeling overwhelmed or lacking confidence in completing tasks. If personal issues are interfering with work, it's advisable to communicate with your manager and consider seeking counseling for support.

Taking care of your physical health is also crucial in managing stress. Addressing any existing health problems and following prescribed medical treatments can help alleviate pain and improve overall well-being, enabling you to better cope with stress. In some cases, it may be necessary to inform your manager about your health conditions to ensure appropriate support and accommodations are provided.

Several factors contribute to stress in the workplace, such as poor communication and organizational difficulties. It's essential to assess the work environment and identify potential stressors, such as being expected to complete tasks without sufficient information. In such situations, don't hesitate to ask for assistance and seek clarification promptly. These proactive strategies can help maintain energy, motivation, and effective health management. They can also be integrated into therapeutic programs aimed at stress reduction.

In addressing stress among social workers, Acceptance and Commitment Therapy has shown promise. Brinkborg et al. (2011) conducted a controlled and randomized trial with social workers experiencing stress. The study found that ACT interventions were effective in reducing stress levels and burnout, with 42% of participants experiencing significant improvement.

The results were particularly impactful for those who initially reported high levels of stress. Overall, ACT was found to be a beneficial short-term intervention for social workers.

Mindfulness-based approaches have also garnered attention for their effectiveness in reducing work-related stress. Bullock (2017) highlighted two studies that explored the impact of mindfulness-based interventions. In one study, executives from a large petroleum jelly firm participated in a mindfulness-based stress reduction program. The program included regular mindfulness exercises, a workbook, and stress management instructions. The study demonstrated reductions in stress levels, improvements in self-efficacy, health, and self-compassion. Blood tests, blood pressure readings, and participant reports confirmed the positive outcomes.

In another study, staff members from two Australian universities underwent a modified mindfulness-based stress reduction program. Participants reported enhanced mindfulness skills, improved sleep quality, and increased overall well-being. While job satisfaction improvements were not significant, participants expressed feeling more relaxed and calmer, experiencing reduced workplace stress, and developing better coping skills. The study also revealed positive effects on family relationships and the ability to disengage from work after hours.

These findings underscore the potential benefits of incorporating mindfulness and stress reduction techniques into the workplace. By embracing these practices and exploring suitable interventions, individuals can cultivate resilience, enhance well-being, and effectively manage stress both inside and outside of work. Remember, each person's experience is unique, so it's essential to find approaches that resonate with you and seek professional guidance when needed.

CHAPTER 16: A COMPARATIVE EXPLORATION OF ACCEPTANCE AND COMMITMENT THERAPY AND DIALECTICAL BEHAVIOR THERAPY

D ialectical behavior therapy (DBT) is a compassionate and collaborative form of Cognitive Behavioral Therapy that focuses on providing support and developing crucial skills for effectively managing intense emotional situations. While initially designed for individuals experiencing suicidal thoughts, DBT has proven beneficial for a variety of conditions involving difficulties in emotional regulation.

DBT encompasses two main components, offering comprehensive support to individuals:

1. Individual weekly therapy sessions: In these one-on-one sessions, patients receive personalized attention and guidance from their therapist. They explore their emotions, challenges, and goals in a safe and non-judgmental environment.

2. Weekly group therapy sessions: Group therapy provides an opportunity for individuals to connect with others who are facing similar struggles. Together, they learn valuable skills, share experiences, and offer mutual support. This group setting fosters a sense of belonging and understanding, reducing feelings of isolation.

By combining individual and group therapy, DBT creates a holistic approach that addresses the unique needs of each individual while also promoting a sense of community and shared growth.

In the journey of mastering essential skills and techniques in DBT, it is important to develop a deep understanding of the following:

Objectiveness effectiveness skills

Describe: Recognizing and articulating your internal feelings is crucial. DBT encourages patients to find the right words that accurately capture their emotions. It's important to remember that emotions can be complex and challenging to express, but by putting them into words, you can gain a better understanding of your own experiences. Describing your feelings helps you communicate effectively with others and seek the support you need.

Express: Patients should feel empowered to express their needs and desires. It's natural to have wants and preferences, and expressing them is an essential part of self-advocacy. When you express your needs, you give yourself a chance to be heard and understood. Don't hesitate to share your thoughts, ideas, and concerns, as they are valuable and deserve to be acknowledged.

Assert: DBT therapy teaches patients to reclaim their power and avoid a victim mentality. Assertiveness allows individuals to confidently express their needs and stand their ground without being aggressive or boastful. It's about finding a balance between being respectful of others and valuing your own opinions and boundaries. Asserting yourself can foster healthy relationships and enhance your self-esteem.

Reinforce: Even the best ideas and plans require reinforcement to become a reality. In the face of challenges, it's important to persevere and support your own efforts. By reinforcing your ideas, actions, and progress, you cultivate resilience and determination. Remember to celebrate your achievements, big or small, as they contribute to your overall growth and well-being.

Mindfulness: Being mindful involves redirecting one's focus to the present moment. Life can be hectic and overwhelming, and it's easy to get caught up in past regrets or future worries. Mindfulness invites you to anchor yourself in the present, embracing the here and now. By practicing mindfulness, you can cultivate a sense of calm, clarity, and gratitude. It's a way of nurturing your mental and emotional well-being amidst the chaos of life.

Confidence: Developing a strong sense of self-esteem is critical. Confidence doesn't guarantee the ability to move mountains, but it equips individuals with a positive mindset that becomes a valuable asset. Self-confidence allows you to believe in your own abilities and worth. It helps you navigate challenges with resilience, embrace new opportunities, and face setbacks with a growth mindset. Cultivating confidence is a journey that involves self-acceptance, self-care, and nurturing your strengths.

Negotiation: DBT empowers patients to recognize their own power and challenge existing norms or ways of doing things. Patients are encouraged to negotiate terms that are favorable to them. Negotiation is not about winning at all costs, but rather finding a middle ground where both parties feel respected and heard. It's about advocating for yourself and finding mutually beneficial solutions. When you engage in negotiation, you cultivate assertiveness, problem-solving skills, and the ability to navigate conflicts with empathy and respect.

In building healthy and effective relationships, DBT encourages the development of relationship effectiveness skills with a compassionate approach. Let's explore some of these skills:

Gentle: DBT emphasizes the importance of approaching your partner with gentleness. Being gentle means being considerate of their feelings, needs, and boundaries. It involves using soft and respectful language, listening attentively, and showing empathy. When you approach your partner with gentleness, they are more likely to respond positively and feel valued in the relationship. Remember, kindness and gentleness can go a long way in nurturing a loving and harmonious connection.

Interested: Showing genuine interest in your partner is a fundamental aspect of maintaining a healthy relationship. It's not enough to assume that your partner knows how much you value them. Actively demonstrate your interest in their life, thoughts, and experiences. Engage in meaningful conversations, ask questions, and actively listen to their responses. By expressing interest, you convey that their presence and opinions matter to you. This fosters a deeper sense of connection and strengthens the bond between you and your partner.

Validate: Contrary to the belief that we don't need validation, validation holds significance in our relationships. We all seek validation from those we hold dear, including our romantic partners. Validating your partner's thoughts, feelings, and experiences shows that you acknowledge and accept them. It's essential to provide validation to your partner, just as you desire to receive it from them. Remember, validation should be genuine and sincere, reinforcing the trust and emotional security within the relationship.

In developing self-respect and practicing self-care, it's important to approach these skills with empathy and compassion. Let's explore some self-respect effectiveness skills from an empathetic perspective:

Fairness: Practicing fairness is not only crucial in our interactions with others but also in how we treat ourselves. It's essential to establish boundaries and prioritize your well-being. Don't let others take advantage of you or disregard your needs. Remember, your self-respect matters, and by being fair to yourself, you set a positive example for others to treat you with the respect you deserve. Balancing fairness towards others and yourself is a step towards building healthy and fulfilling relationships.

Apologies: It's inevitable that we will encounter challenging situations and conflicts with others. If you find yourself in the wrong, offering a sincere apology demonstrates humility and a willingness to take responsibility for your actions. On the other hand, if you've been wronged, seeking an apology shows that you value fairness and resolution. While receiving an unsolicited apology may be ideal, acknowledging the other person's goodwill can be a step towards reconciliation and healing.

Truthfulness: Honesty is a powerful virtue that extends not only to others but also to yourself. Being truthful with yourself and others fosters trust, authenticity, and healthy communication. It may not always be easy, but embracing the truth simplifies your life and helps you build genuine connections. Remember, by honoring the truth, you cultivate a sense of integrity and self-respect that contributes to your overall well-being.

When it comes to Acceptance and Commitment Therapy, the focus is on enhancing psychological flexibility and cultivating present-moment awareness. Let's explore a couple of principles of ACT with an empathetic lens:

Acceptance: Each person experiences negative thoughts and emotions to varying degrees. It's natural to want to push away these unpleasant experiences, but ACT encourages patients to accept them. By making room for these feelings, urges, and sensations, individuals can develop a more compassionate and non-judgmental relationship with themselves. Embracing an abundance mindset allows for the release of negative patterns that have held them captive.

Cognitive Defusion: Cognitive defusion involves perceiving thoughts, words, images, and other mental activities as stand-alone experiences. Instead of getting caught up in the meanings and stories attached to these cognitions, ACT encourages individuals to observe them without fusion. For example, the simple phrase "chocolate cake" might evoke strong cravings and imagery. By practicing cognitive defusion, patients can observe these thoughts without getting entangled in their power, allowing for greater psychological flexibility and reduced reactivity.

Approaching self-respect and Acceptance and Commitment Therapy with empathy and understanding allows individuals to navigate their inner experiences with kindness and compassion. Remember, self-care and psychological growth are ongoing processes that require patience and self-compassion. By embracing these skills and principles, individuals can foster a healthier and more fulfilling relationship with themselves and the world around them.

CHAPTER 17: ACT STRATEGIES FOR REDUCING OCD SYMPTOMS

This chapter explores the application of Acceptance and Commitment Therapy in managing Obsessive-Compulsive Disorder (OCD). Topics covered include Exposure and Response Prevention (ERP), Thought Stopping, Thought Labeling, and Expansion and Acceptance. ACT incorporates principles of behavioral psychology and mindfulness, emphasizing language and cognition's role in psychopathology. The chapter discusses behavior change techniques based on operant conditioning and traditional behavior therapy methods. ACT offers a unique approach to OCD treatment, focusing on acceptance and commitment to valued actions.

Exposure and Response Prevention (ERP) is a highly effective form of Cognitive Behavioral Therapy that has been widely used in the treatment of Obsessive-Compulsive Disorder. The core principle of ERP revolves around gradually exposing individuals to their fears or triggers, while simultaneously preventing the usual compulsive responses that typically alleviate anxiety.

Engaging in ERP requires immense courage and strength on the part of individuals with OCD. It involves facing deeply unsettling and distressing thoughts, images, or situations in a controlled and supportive therapeutic environment. The therapist guides the individual through the process, providing reassurance and encouragement along the way. This empathetic approach acknowledges the inherent difficulties of confronting one's fears head-on and recognizes the immense bravery it takes to endure the accompanying anxiety.

By confronting their fears in a gradual and systematic manner, individuals undergoing ERP learn to tolerate the distress and anxiety triggered by their obsessions. Through repeated exposure, they gradually discover that their anxiety naturally diminishes over time, without resorting to compulsive behaviors. This process of desensitization helps individuals gain a sense of control over their anxiety and reduces the need for repetitive rituals or mental compulsions.

It is essential for therapists and treatment providers to approach ERP with empathy and understanding. They play a crucial role in providing a safe and supportive environment where individuals can openly express their fears, anxieties, and discomfort. Therapists work collaboratively with their clients, tailoring the exposure exercises to their specific fears and triggers. The empathetic stance adopted by therapists fosters trust, allows for open communication, and empowers individuals to confront their OCD symptoms with greater confidence.

Thought Stopping

Thought Stopping is a cognitive-behavioral technique used to interrupt and replace unwanted or distressing thoughts. It aims to disrupt negative thinking patterns and prevent the escalation of unhelpful thoughts that can contribute to anxiety, worry, or other mental health issues. Thought Stopping involves actively blocking the unwanted thought and replacing it with a more positive or neutral thought. By using this technique, individuals can gain greater control over their thoughts and reduce the impact of negative thinking on their emotions and behaviors.

I'll walk you through the exercise:

a. Identify the unwanted or distressing thought that you want to stop. It could be a negative self-critical thought, an intrusive worry, or any thought that is causing distress.

b. Visualize a stop sign or create a mental image of the word "Stop" whenever the unwanted thought arises in your mind.

c. As soon as you notice the unwanted thought, mentally shout "Stop!" or imagine yourself pressing a pause button to interrupt the thought.

d. Take a deep breath and redirect your attention to a more positive or neutral thought. This could be a calming image, a happy memory, or a statement that counters the negative thought.

e. Repeat this process whenever the unwanted thought resurfaces. Practice consistency and persistence in stopping and replacing the thought.

Key Takeaways and Next Steps

- It's important to note that Thought Stopping may not completely eliminate unwanted thoughts but aims to disrupt their impact and reduce their frequency over time.

- Consistent practice is key to mastering this technique. It may feel challenging at first, but with time and persistence, it can become more automatic.

- Be patient and kind to yourself. It's natural for unwanted thoughts to arise, and it takes time to change thought patterns.

- Combine Thought Stopping with other therapeutic techniques, such as cognitive restructuring or mindfulness, to enhance its effectiveness.

- If you find it difficult to implement Thought Stopping on your own, consider seeking guidance from a mental health professional who can provide further support and tailor the technique to your specific needs.

Thought Labeling

Thought Labeling is a technique used in various therapeutic approaches, including Acceptance and Commitment Therapy, to help individuals gain distance from their thoughts and reduce their impact. It involves recognizing and labeling thoughts as just thoughts, without attaching excessive importance or validity to them. By practicing Thought Labeling, you can develop a more mindful and detached perspective towards your thoughts, allowing you to respond to them more effectively.

Here's how you do the exercise:

a. Find a quiet and comfortable space where you can sit or lie down without distractions.

173

b. Close your eyes and take a few deep breaths to center yourself and bring your attention to the present moment.

c. Begin to observe your thoughts as they arise in your mind. Notice any recurring patterns or themes.

d. Whenever you become aware of a thought, mentally label it as "thought" or "thinking."

e. Avoid getting caught up in the content of the thought or engaging in judgment or analysis. Simply acknowledge its presence and let it go.

f. If your mind starts to wander or gets caught up in a particular thought, gently bring your attention back to the present moment and continue observing your thoughts without attachment.

g. Practice this exercise for a few minutes each day, gradually increasing the duration as you become more comfortable with the process.

Tips for Execution

- Remember that the purpose of Thought Labeling is not to suppress or eliminate thoughts but to develop a more mindful and non-reactive stance towards them.

- Be patient with yourself. It takes time and practice to

cultivate the skill of observing thoughts without getting caught up in their content.

- Notice any judgments or self-criticism that may arise during the practice. Treat yourself with kindness and self-compassion, acknowledging that thoughts are a natural part of the human experience.

- You can combine Thought Labeling with other mindfulness techniques, such as focused breathing or body scan meditation, to enhance your overall mindfulness practice.

- It can be helpful to work with a qualified therapist or counselor who specializes in OCD or ACT to receive guidance and support in applying Thought Labeling and other techniques effectively.

Expansion and Acceptance

Expansion and acceptance, as it relates to psychological well-being and personal growth, involves creating space for difficult emotions, thoughts, and experiences while maintaining a willingness to engage in meaningful actions aligned with one's values. It is a key concept in various therapeutic approaches, including Acceptance and Commitment Therapy.

Here's a step-by-step exercise to practice expansion and acceptance:

Step 1: Identify a challenging or distressing thought or emotion that you commonly experience.

Step 2: Take a few moments to bring your attention to this thought or emotion. Notice its presence without judgment.

Step 3: Allow the thought or emotion to expand in your awareness. Notice any physical sensations or accompanying thoughts that arise.

Step 4: As you observe the thought or emotion, remind yourself that it is simply a passing experience and not a reflection of your worth or identity.

Step 5: Breathe deeply and anchor yourself in the present moment. Bring your attention to your breath or the sensations in your body.

Step 6: Connect with your values and consider what actions align with what truly matters to you in this situation.

Step 7: Make a commitment to engage in a valued action, even in the presence of discomfort or challenging thoughts and emotions.

Keep in mind that this exercise may take practice and patience. The goal is not to eliminate difficult experiences but to develop a different relationship with them, allowing you to live a meaningful life.

I hope you found this chapter helpful. Acceptance and Commitment Therapy can help people with OCD to develop psychological flexibility, which is the ability to accept difficult thoughts and feelings without letting them control their behavior. This can lead to a significant improvement in quality of life.

CHAPTER 18: CULTIVATING MINDFULNESS THROUGH PRACTICAL EXERCISES

T hroughout this chapter, we will delve into practical techniques and exercises that can seamlessly integrate into our daily routines. These practices offer valuable opportunities to tap into the richness of the present and awaken a heightened sense of self-awareness. Whether you are new to mindfulness or have already embraced its benefits, the insights and guidance within this chapter will support you in nurturing mindfulness as a way of life.

Together, we will explore the art of mindful living and discover how these practices can help us navigate the complexities of our modern world with greater ease and equanimity. By dedicating ourselves to these exercises, we open ourselves to the transformative power of mindfulness, allowing it to enhance our mental, emotional, and physical well-being.

Join us as we embark on this exploration of mindfulness in daily life, discovering the potential it holds to bring greater peace, clarity, and fulfillment. Through these practical tools, we will uncover the beauty of living fully in each passing moment and embrace the profound benefits that mindfulness can bring.

So, take a deep breath, open your heart to the present, and let us embark on this journey of self-discovery and mindful living. Together, we will unlock the potential of mindfulness and cultivate a deeper sense of connection, contentment, and authenticity in our lives.

Mindful Breathing

Mindful breathing is a simple yet powerful exercise that allows you to anchor your attention to the present moment by focusing on your breath. It is a foundational practice in mindfulness and is often used to cultivate awareness, calm the mind, and reduce stress. By directing your attention to the physical sensations of your breath, you can develop a greater sense of presence and engage with the present moment more fully.

To practice mindful breathing, follow these practical steps:

a) Find a Quiet Space: Begin by finding a quiet and comfortable space where you can sit or lie down without any distractions. It could be a peaceful corner of your home, a serene outdoor spot, or any place where you feel at ease. Creating a conducive environment for your practice allows you to fully engage with the exercise.

b) Get Centered: Take a few moments to settle into your body and bring your awareness to the present moment. You can do this by gently closing your eyes or softly focusing your gaze. Allow yourself to let go of any thoughts, worries, or responsibilities from the past or future. This is your dedicated time to be fully present with yourself.

c) Focus on the Breath: Direct your attention to the sensation of your breath entering and leaving your body. Notice the natural flow of your breath, whether it's through your nostrils, chest, or abdomen. You can place one hand on your belly to feel the rise and fall, or simply observe the air passing through your nostrils. Choose an anchor point that feels most comfortable for you.

d) Stay Present: As you continue to focus on your breath, you may find that your mind starts to wander or get caught up in thoughts. It's normal for this to happen. When you become aware that your mind has drifted, gently and non-judgmentally guide your attention back to the breath. Acknowledge the thoughts without getting entangled in them, and gently refocus your attention on the present moment.

e) Observe Sensations: As you engage in mindful breathing, you may notice various physical sensations associated with your breath. Pay attention to the temperature of the air, the movement of your body, or any other sensations that arise. Allow yourself to experience these sensations fully, without judgment or the need to change them. Each breath is a unique experience, and you can fully immerse yourself in the present moment through these sensations.

f) Practice Regularly: Aim to incorporate mindful breathing into your daily routine. Start with shorter durations, such as 5-10 minutes, and gradually increase the length of your practice over time. Consistency is key in reaping the benefits of this exercise. Consider setting a specific time each day for your mindful breathing practice, whether it's in the morning to start your day with clarity or in the evening to unwind and relax before bed.

By consistently engaging in mindful breathing, you can develop a greater capacity for present-moment awareness and a more grounded connection to your breath. This exercise can serve as an anchor during challenging moments, providing a sense of calm and stability. Remember to approach this practice with patience and self-compassion, allowing yourself to fully experience the present moment through the rhythm of your breath.

Values Clarification

Values clarification is a process of exploring and defining your core values—the guiding principles and qualities that hold deep meaning and significance in your life. By gaining clarity about your values, you can align your actions and choices with what truly matters to you. This exercise helps you connect with your authentic self and provides a compass for making decisions that are in line with your values.

Practical Steps to Perform Values Clarification:

a) Create a Reflective Space: Find a quiet and comfortable space where you can reflect without interruptions. It could be a cozy corner in your home, a peaceful park, or any place where you feel at ease. Creating a conducive environment allows you to engage in self-reflection with focus and intention.

b) Reflect on Different Life Areas: Begin by considering different areas of your life, such as relationships, work, health, personal growth, spirituality, or any other aspect that holds importance to you. Take a moment to think about what values are relevant in each area and how they contribute to your overall well-being and fulfillment.

c) Identify Core Values: As you reflect on each life area, ask yourself what qualities, principles, or virtues are most important to you in that particular domain. For example, in relationships, you may value trust, respect, empathy, or authenticity. Write down these core values as they come to mind, allowing yourself to express them freely without judgment.

d) Prioritize Your Values: Once you have identified several core values, prioritize them based on their significance and impact on your life. Consider which values resonate with you on a deep level and align with your sense of purpose and fulfillment. You may find that some values are more central and influential, while others may hold a secondary or supporting role.

e) Write Them Down: Take a pen and paper or use a digital tool to write down your core values. Create a list that you can refer to regularly. Seeing your values in written form reinforces their importance and helps you stay connected to them in your daily life. Consider placing your list somewhere visible, such as on your desk or as a screensaver on your electronic devices.

f) Revisit and Reflect: Set aside time periodically to revisit and reflect on your values. This could be weekly, monthly, or whenever you feel the need to reconnect with what truly matters to you. Review your values, consider how they are influencing your choices and actions, and reflect on any adjustments or realignments you may want to make.

g) Integrate Values into Decision-Making: Use your values as a compass when making decisions. When faced with choices or dilemmas, consider how each option aligns with your core values. Ask yourself which option supports and upholds what you truly value. This process can guide you towards decisions that are in harmony with your authentic self and lead to greater satisfaction and fulfillment.

Defusion Techniques

Defusion techniques are a core component of Acceptance and Commitment Therapy (ACT) aimed at helping individuals create distance from their unhelpful thoughts. The goal is not to eliminate or control thoughts but to change our relationship with them, allowing us to observe them without getting entangled or overwhelmed. This exercise promotes psychological flexibility and empowers us to choose how we respond to our thoughts.

Practical Steps to Perform Defusion Techniques:

a) Labeling Thoughts as "Just Thoughts": Begin by recognizing that thoughts are simply mental events and not necessarily an accurate reflection of reality. When a challenging or distressing thought arises, practice labeling it as "just a thought." This simple acknowledgment reminds you that thoughts come and go and do not define who you are or dictate your actions. It creates space between you and the thought, allowing you to observe it with a sense of detachment.

b) Observing Thoughts without Judgment: Once you've labeled a thought as "just a thought," shift your focus to observing it without judgment. Notice the thought without attaching meaning or significance to it. Imagine yourself as an impartial observer watching thoughts pass by like clouds in the sky. By cultivating this detached perspective, you can prevent thoughts from triggering strong emotional reactions or influencing your behavior.

c) Silly Voice Technique: Another defusion technique involves repeating challenging thoughts in a silly or comical voice. By giving your thoughts an amusing twist, you decrease their impact and power over you. It helps to create a lighthearted atmosphere and diminishes the seriousness or heaviness associated with the thought. This technique can bring a sense of playfulness and lightness to your internal dialogue.

d) Singing Thoughts to a Familiar Tune: Similar to the silly voice technique, singing your challenging thoughts to a familiar tune can also reduce their intensity. Choose a melody that you know well and adapt the lyrics to match the content of the thought. By transforming the thought into a song, you engage your creative side and create distance from the thought's emotional grip. Singing adds an element of lightness and shifts your focus away from the distressing nature of the thought.

e) Practice and Integration: Regularly incorporate defusion techniques into your daily routine. Whenever unhelpful thoughts arise, apply the labeling, observation, silly voice, or singing techniques. Over time, these practices become more natural and ingrained, empowering you to defuse from unhelpful thoughts effectively. Remember that like any skill, defusion techniques require practice and patience. Be gentle with yourself and embrace the learning process.

Daily Committed Action

Daily committed action is an essential practice in Acceptance and Commitment Therapy (ACT) that involves taking small, meaningful steps aligned with your values on a consistent basis. By engaging in actions that reflect what truly matters to you, you cultivate a sense of purpose, fulfillment, and alignment with your values. This exercise empowers you to make deliberate choices and actively shape your life according to your deepest aspirations.

Practical Steps to Perform Daily Committed Action:

a) Reflect on Your Values: Begin by reflecting on your core values in different areas of your life, such as relationships, work, health, personal growth, or community involvement. Identify what truly matters to you and what you want to prioritize. Consider qualities, principles, and actions that are in line with these values. This introspective process helps you gain clarity on the actions you can commit to daily.

b) Choose a Small Action: Select a small action that you can easily incorporate into your daily routine. It can be as simple as expressing gratitude, engaging in a hobby or creative outlet, engaging in self-care activities, or reaching out to a loved one. The key is to choose something that aligns with your values and is achievable within your current circumstances. Starting small allows you to build momentum and create a habit of consistent action.

c) Set a Daily Reminder: Create a reminder or cue that prompts you to engage in your chosen action each day. It can be a notification on your phone, a sticky note in a visible location, or associating the action with an existing daily routine. Setting a reminder helps to establish a consistent habit and ensures that you prioritize the action amidst the busyness of daily life.

d) Integrate Mindfulness: As you engage in your daily committed action, bring a sense of mindfulness to the experience. Be fully present and attentive to the activity, savoring each moment and immersing yourself in the process. Allow yourself to appreciate the significance of the action and how it aligns with your values. Mindfulness enhances your connection with the action and amplifies its impact on your overall well-being.

e) Track Your Progress: Keep a record of your daily committed actions. It can be a simple journal where you write down the action you took each day. Tracking your progress not only provides a sense of accomplishment but also serves as a reminder of the consistency and dedication you bring to your values. Reflecting on your progress over time can be motivating and encouraging.

f) Adjust and Expand: As you become comfortable with your chosen daily committed action, consider expanding or exploring new actions that align with your values. You can gradually increase the complexity or time spent on the action or explore different actions altogether. The goal is to continuously grow and adapt your daily committed actions to reflect your evolving values and aspirations.

Self-Compassion Practice

Self-compassion is a vital aspect of Acceptance and Commitment Therapy that involves cultivating kindness, understanding, and acceptance towards oneself. It is the act of treating yourself with the same warmth and care that you would extend to a dear friend in times of difficulty. By practicing self-compassion, you develop a nurturing and supportive relationship with yourself, fostering resilience, emotional well-being, and personal growth.

Practical Steps to Perform Self-Compassion Practice:

a) Cultivate Awareness: Begin by cultivating awareness of your self-talk and internal dialogue. Notice the tone and language you use when speaking to yourself, particularly in challenging or critical situations. Becoming aware of your self-critical thoughts and judgments is the first step towards practicing self-compassion.

b) Kindness and Understanding: When faced with difficult emotions or setbacks, consciously shift your inner dialogue to one of kindness and understanding. Treat yourself as you would treat a dear friend or loved one. Offer yourself words of encouragement, support, and comfort. Remind yourself that experiencing challenges and setbacks is a natural part of being human.

c) Embrace Imperfections: Recognize and embrace your imperfections and limitations. Understand that nobody is perfect, and making mistakes is an inevitable part of growth and learning. Instead of judging yourself harshly, practice self-acceptance and remind yourself that you are worthy and deserving of compassion, regardless of your perceived flaws.

d) Practice Self-Compassionate Language: Use self-compassionate language when speaking to yourself. Instead of berating yourself for mistakes, offer words of understanding and encouragement. For example, instead of saying, "I'm such a failure," reframe it as, "I'm doing my best, and it's okay to make mistakes."

e) Mindful Self-Compassion: Combine self-compassion with mindfulness by bringing awareness to your present moment experience. When facing challenging emotions or thoughts, practice non-judgmental observation and acceptance. Allow yourself to fully acknowledge and experience your feelings without judgment or resistance.

f) Self-Compassion Breaks: Take intentional self-compassion breaks throughout the day. These are short moments where you pause, acknowledge your struggles, and offer yourself compassion. You can say phrases like, "May I be kind to myself in this moment" or "May I give myself the compassion I need."

g) Self-Compassion Rituals: Incorporate self-compassion into your daily routine through small rituals. It can be as simple as taking a few minutes each morning to reflect on your intentions for self-compassion or engaging in activities that bring you joy and nourishment. These rituals reinforce the practice of self-compassion and create a supportive environment for your well-being.

h) Cultivate a Supportive Inner Voice: Develop a supportive and nurturing inner voice that encourages self-compassion. Imagine a compassionate figure or mentor and visualize them offering you words of kindness and understanding. Use this visualization to strengthen your own self-compassionate voice.

Observing Your Thoughts and Emotions

In Acceptance and Commitment Therapy, the practice of observing thoughts and emotions without judgment is a fundamental skill. It involves cultivating a mindful awareness of your internal experiences, allowing you to observe them with curiosity and openness. By developing this skill, you can create distance from your thoughts and emotions, gain insight into their patterns, and cultivate a more accepting and compassionate relationship with yourself.

Practical Steps to Perform Observing Your Thoughts and Emotions:

a) Cultivate Mindful Awareness: Set aside dedicated moments throughout the day to cultivate mindful awareness of your thoughts and emotions. Find a quiet space where you can sit comfortably and bring your attention to the present moment. Allow yourself to become fully aware of your thoughts, emotions, and bodily sensations without trying to change or judge them.

b) Non-Judgmental Observation: As you observe your thoughts and emotions, practice non-judgmental observation. Instead of labeling thoughts as "good" or "bad," simply notice them as mental events passing through your awareness. Be curious about their content, intensity, and frequency without getting caught up in their storylines.

c) Detachment from Thoughts: Recognize that thoughts are not facts or truths. They are mental events that arise and fade away. Practice seeing your thoughts as separate from yourself, like clouds passing through the sky. By cultivating this sense of detachment, you create space between you and your thoughts, allowing for a more objective and balanced perspective.

d) Curiosity and Inquiry: Approach your thoughts and emotions with a sense of curiosity and inquiry. Ask yourself questions like "What is the underlying emotion behind this thought?" or "What patterns or themes do I notice in my thinking?" This curiosity allows you to gain insights into your internal experiences and identify any unhelpful patterns or recurring themes.

e) Radical Acceptance: Practice accepting your thoughts and emotions as they are, without trying to change or resist them. Recognize that all thoughts and emotions are valid and part of the human experience. Embrace them with a compassionate and non-judgmental attitude, allowing them to come and go without attachment.

f) Breathing Space: When you notice yourself becoming overwhelmed or caught up in your thoughts and emotions, take a brief pause to create a breathing space. Close your eyes if it feels comfortable, take a few deep breaths, and bring your attention to the physical sensation of your breath. This simple practice helps ground you in the present moment and provides a break from the automatic reactivity to your internal experiences.

g) Journaling: Consider keeping a journal to record your observations of thoughts and emotions. Write down any patterns, themes, or insights that arise during your practice. Journaling provides a tangible way to reflect on your internal experiences and track your progress over time.

h) Integration into Daily Life: Extend the practice of observing your thoughts and emotions into your daily life. Whenever you find yourself caught up in unhelpful thoughts or overwhelmed by emotions, take a step back and observe them from a more detached perspective. This practice helps you cultivate a more mindful and accepting stance towards your internal experiences, enhancing your overall well-being.

Mindful Walking

Mindful walking is a simple yet powerful practice that allows you to bring mindfulness into your everyday movements. It involves paying deliberate attention to the physical sensations and experiences associated with each step you take. By engaging in mindful walking, you can anchor yourself in the present moment, deepen your connection with your body, and cultivate a sense of groundedness and awareness.

Practical Steps to Perform Mindful Walking:

a) Choose a Walking Path: Find a safe and quiet place where you can engage in mindful walking. It can be indoors or outdoors, depending on your preference and accessibility. Ensure that the path is free from obstacles or distractions that may disrupt your focus.

b) Set an Intention: Before you begin, set an intention to cultivate mindfulness and present-moment awareness during your walking practice. Remind yourself that this is a dedicated time to focus on the physical sensations of walking and to let go of any distractions or worries.

c) Start with Stillness: Begin by standing still for a moment, grounding yourself in the present moment. Feel the contact of your feet on the ground, bring your awareness to your breath, and allow any tension or stress to release from your body.

d) Attune to Sensations: As you start walking, shift your attention to the physical sensations of walking. Notice the feeling of your feet lifting off the ground, the movement of your legs, and the contact between your feet and the surface beneath you. Observe the sensations of your muscles, joints, and the subtle shifts in balance as you take each step.

e) Cultivate Body Awareness: Pay attention to the various parts of your body involved in walking. Notice how your arms swing naturally by your side, the alignment of your spine, and the engagement of your core muscles. Bring your awareness to the sensations in your feet, such as the pressure, temperature, and texture of the ground beneath them.

f) Stay Present: As you continue walking, practice staying present in the current moment. Allow any distracting thoughts or worries to pass by without attaching to them. If your mind wanders, gently guide your attention back to the physical sensations of walking, anchoring yourself in the present experience.

g) Engage Your Senses: Expand your awareness to the environment around you. Notice the sights, sounds, and smells as you walk. Observe the colors, shapes, and textures of your surroundings. Engaging your senses helps deepen your connection with the present moment and enhances your overall experience of mindful walking.

h) Gentle and Natural Pace: Maintain a gentle and natural pace that feels comfortable to you. Mindful walking is not about speed or reaching a specific destination; it's about being fully present with each step. Allow yourself to move at a pace that allows you to savor the experience and maintain a sense of ease and relaxation.

i) Open Awareness: As you near the end of your walking practice, gradually expand your awareness to include your body as a whole and the overall experience of walking. Notice any changes in your breath, energy levels, or emotional state. Take a moment to appreciate the practice and the opportunity to connect with your body and the present moment.

j) Carry Mindfulness into Daily Life: Extend the practice of mindful walking beyond your dedicated sessions. Find moments throughout your day to bring mindfulness to your steps, whether it's walking from one room to another or taking a stroll in nature. By integrating mindful walking into your daily life, you enhance your ability to stay present and grounded amidst the busyness of everyday activities.

CONCLUSION

A s we reach the conclusion of our shared exploration, I extend my heartfelt appreciation to you for joining me on this transformative path. Throughout our time together, we have ventured into the depths of Acceptance and Commitment Therapy, unraveling its profound insights and practical applications. Now, let us recap our voyage, capturing the essence of our discussions and offering you a lasting reservoir of wisdom to carry forward.

In our pursuit of personal growth and well-being, we embarked on an odyssey through the realms of ACT, an approach that invites us to embrace acceptance, mindfulness, and committed action. We discovered that ACT is not merely a collection of techniques but a philosophy—a way of being—that empowers us to live in harmony with our values and navigate the ebbs and flows of life's challenges.

With empathy and compassion as our guides, we delved into the core processes of ACT. We explored the power of acceptance, cultivating the capacity to acknowledge our thoughts, emotions, and experiences with tenderness and non-judgment. Through the lens of mindfulness, we deepened our connection with the present moment, unshackling ourselves from the weight of past regrets and the pull of future uncertainties.

Our journey led us to the transformative potential of committed action. By aligning our actions with our deepest values, we unearthed a path of purpose and fulfillment. We recognized the significance of self-compassion and self-care, understanding that our well-being radiates beyond ourselves, nourishing the relationships we cherish and the communities we inhabit.

Amidst our exploration, we encountered the stories and insights of fellow travelers who, like us, have embarked on their own quests for growth and resilience. Their narratives serve as poignant reminders that we are not solitary seekers but interconnected souls, each contributing to the tapestry of human experience with our unique threads.

As we conclude this book, I wish to express my sincere gratitude to you, dear reader. Thank you for accompanying me on this profound voyage of self-discovery and introspection. Your dedication to your own well-being is a testament to your courage, and I hope the knowledge and insights we have uncovered together will continue to guide you on your path.

Remember, personal growth is not an arrival but an ongoing pilgrimage. I encourage you to revisit the pages of this book, allowing its wisdom to permeate your everyday existence. Embrace the practices of acceptance and mindfulness, anchoring yourself in the present moment. Harness the transformative power of committed action as you step forward on a purpose-driven journey.

In closing, I extend my warmest wishes to you. May you nurture your mental health and well-being with unwavering compassion and care. May you face life's trials with resilience and seek support when needed, knowing that you are not alone in your endeavors. Together, let us foster a world rooted in compassion and flourishing.

Thank you for accompanying me on this chapter of our shared voyage. May this book serve as a trusted companion, offering solace, guidance, and inspiration whenever you seek it. Until our paths converge again, whether within these pages or in the ever-unfolding tapestry of life, take care, be gentle with yourself, and embrace the transformative essence of ACT.

Milton Keynes UK
Ingram Content Group UK Ltd.
UKHW020820280823
427620UK00015B/725